PRACTICAL HOUSEHOLD USES OF
VINEGAR

D1230876

PRACTICAL HOUSEHOLD USES OF
VINEGAR

HOME CURES, RECIPES,
EVERYDAY HINTS AND TIPS

MARGARET BRIGGS

southwater

This edition is published by Southwater

an imprint of Anness Publishing Ltd

Blaby Road, Wigston

Leicestershire LE18 4SE

info@anness.com

www.southwaterbooks.com

www.annesspublishing.com

© Anness Publishing Ltd 2013

A CIP catalogue record for this book
is available from the British Library.

Publisher: Joanna Lorenz
Senior Editor: Felicity Forster
Cover Design: Nigel Partridge
Production Controller: Wendy Lawson

PUBLISHER'S NOTE
Although the advice and information in this book are
believed to be accurate and true at the time of going to
press, neither the authors nor the publisher can accept any
legal responsibility or liability for any errors or omissions
that may have been made nor for any inaccuracies nor for
any loss, harm or injury that comes about from following
instructions or advice in this book.

CONTENTS

Introduction

It's amazing that a product discovered by accident more than 10,000 years ago is still used so widely today — and for such a wide range of purposes. Anyone who has ever left a bottle of wine uncorked (with wine still in it) will know what happens. That's not a problem for some of us, as wine bottles are emptied quite promptly! However, under the effects of bacteria, the alcohol is turned into acetic acid, better known as vinegar. Even Louis Pasteur has a place in the story. His invention of pasteurization of milk came about indirectly, after he was employed by the wine-making industry to find out why wine went off so quickly.

What would the British do without vinegar on their fish and chips? Despite the cries of laughter and derision from continental friends, turning to disgust as we put a generous dousing of vinegar on to one of the nation's favourite dishes, there's a sound reason for doing so, and it's not just to make the chips taste better.

Look in any Victorian household management book, for example, the works of Mrs Beeton, and you will see endless recipes for flavoured vinegars, as well as a dazzling array of applications in cleaning, laundry and home medicine.

As recently as World War I, vinegar was being used to treat wounds. Today it is recommended for treatment of rashes, bites and other minor ailments.

Throughout history there have been countless civilizations which have been aware of the wide ranging benefits of vinegar to the palate, to hygiene and to the pocket. Here is a staple from your pantry shelf — economical, always at hand, ready to serve in a variety of ways. One bottle of white distilled vinegar contains a whole shelf's worth of specialized cleaners.

This book provides a short summary of vinegar through the ages and differences from other cultures. It also gives a comprehensive list of the many practical and money-saving hints, tips and recipes which you may find invaluable around the home.

A Short History of Vinegar

Ancient civilizations were quick to recognize the versatility of vinegar. The Babylonians used it as a preservative and Roman legionnaires used it as a beverage. Cleopatra demonstrated its solvent properties to win a bet, Hippocrates extolled its medicinal qualities and when Hannibal crossed the Alps, it was vinegar which helped pave the way. Was vinegar the world's first bulldozer?

EARLY MULTI-PURPOSE PANACEA

Vinegar has a 10,000 year history, dating from the production of alcoholic drinks — beer, wine and other spirits. Vinegar is a natural by-product of alcoholic beverages and its discovery was almost certainly accidental. People made the discovery in different parts of the world independently, and for as long as there have been undistilled, alcoholic drinks, there has been vinegar. Ancient civilizations as far back as the Sumerians used vinegar as a condiment, a preservative, a medicine, an antibiotic and a detergent, just as we do today.

BABYLONIAN BEVERAGE

The earliest written record is 5,000 BC when the Babylonians made vinegar by fermenting the fruit of date palms. An old Babylonian saying that 'Beer that went sour wandered into the kitchen' suggests that these early people used vinegar when cooking.

RELIGIOUS REFERENCES

Vinegar is mentioned in the Bible, in both the Old and New Testaments — in the Book of Ruth and in Proverbs. It is also specifically called for in the making of haroseth in Pesachim, a section of the Talmud, the Jewish book of civil and ceremonial law.

ROMAN REFRESHMENT

The word vinegar comes from the Latin word *vinum* meaning wine and *acer* meaning sour. The French word *vinaigre* derives from Latin. The word *alegar* was used for vinegar made from ale or beer. The

Romans made vinegar from grapes, figs, dates and rye. The armies of Julius Caesar would drink Posca, a refreshing mixture of water and vinegar, as part of every meal and for its antiseptic properties.

PHILOSOPHICAL PANACEA

Hippocrates, the father of medicine, prescribed the drinking of vinegar for his patients in ancient Greece. Many ancient cultures used vinegar and valued it for its medicinal benefits. Aristotle and Sophocles also made reference to uses of vinegar.

MOLEHILLS FROM MOUNTAINS

Without vinegar, Hannibal's march over the Alps to Rome may not have been possible. The chronicles of Livy describing this historic march include the essential role vinegar played in the task of getting Hannibal's elephants over perilous mountain trails.

Frequently, the passes across the Alps were too narrow for the huge elephants. Hannibal's solution was to cut branches and stack them around the boulders which blocked their way. Soldiers then set the wood on fire. When the rocks were good and hot, vinegar was poured on to them, turning the stones soft and crumbly. The soldiers could then chip the rocks away, making a passage for both the troops and elephants.

EGYPTIAN ENIGMA

Many paintings discovered in Egyptian burial tombs from the 11th and 13th dynasty show people busy brewing. Legend has it that Cleopatra made her own entry into the vinegar history book by making a wager with Anthony that she could consume a meal worth a million sesterces, which represented a great huge amount of wealth.

How did she go about winning her bet? At the start of the banquet, she placed a valuable pearl in a vase filled with vinegar then at the end of the meal she drank the liquid in which the pearl had dissolved! Sadly the act did her no good as she was arrested soon after and stripped of all her assets.

CRYPTEX CRACKER
Leonardo Da Vinci knew about the effects of vinegar on papyrus and invented an ingenious mechanical device to allow secret, coded messages to be sent without being read if intercepted. In his novel, entitled *The Da Vinci Code*, Dan Brown uses Leonardo's cryptex idea to hide a map around a phial of vinegar. If the phial broke, the vinegar would dissolve the papyrus and the information written on it.

ALL KINDS OF ALCHEMY
Alchemists were interested in vinegar from early times and the vinegar-makers jealously guarded their manufacturing secrets. For centuries, the first concern was to accelerate its production, and there were so many recipes that the vinegar makers remarked that living material accelerated the acidification. From then on anything was possible: vine shoots, brambles, vegetables, even fish tongues were thrown into the wine!

CHINESE CHENCU
Meanwhile, in China a different form of vinegar was developed from rice water. Chencu, or mature vinegar, has been used as a kind of flavouring for more than 1000 years.

BALSAMIC BIRTHPLACE
The first literary references to balsamic vinegar date back to the year 1046. In that year Emperor Henry III went from northern Europe to Rome. On the way, while stopping in Piacenza, he asked Marquis Bonifacio for a small cask of the famous laudatum acentum.

Further documentary proof confirms Modena as the birthplace of balsamic vinegar, whose method of preparation did not undergo any significant changes for many centuries. The traditional raw material for balsamic vinegar had always been wine vinegar, which was aged for hundreds of years. In 1861 Mr. Aggazzotti, a lawyer, introduced a revolutionary production technique that used concentrated grape must as the raw material instead of wine vinegar. This is the method that has been used ever since to produce traditional balsamic vinegars.

VINEGAR-MAKERS WORTH THEIR SALT

From the reign of Charles VI, the occupation of vinegar-distilling was made into a corporation which was first registered in October 1394, in Paris. The statutes were completed in 1514 making up a trade body under the official title of 'Vinegar-makers, mustard and sauce-makers, brandy liqueur and rectified spirit distillers'. Workers in this trade had to be 'sound in limb and clean in dress'.

PLAGUE POTION

During the middle ages, vinegar was heavily used, not only as a drink and condiment, but also for washing and for treating many illnesses such as the plague, leprosy, fever and snake bites. As fear and chaos reigned during these plagues, people performed odd and cruel rituals to spare their town.

In some towns and villages in England there are still the old market crosses which have a depression at the foot of the stone cross. This was filled with vinegar during times of plague, as it was believed that vinegar would kill any germs on the coins and so contain the disease.

FOUR THIEVES

Legends also abounded about those who survived, in particular, four thieves who robbed the bodies and houses of the dead but did not contract the illness. The legend places the thieves in Marseilles, or Toulouse, or perhaps London, during the plague epidemic which ravaged Europe during the 17th century. In 1628, 1632, or 1722, they were caught and sentenced to death, but were told they would be spared if they revealed the secret for their survival: the Vinegar of Four Thieves.

Some recipes called for red wine vinegar, others for cider vinegar, mixed with herbs-lavender blossoms, rue, rosemary, sage; some added wormwood, thyme, mint, and garlic, and the vinegar was either steeped in the sun or buried in a crock. The unfortunate victims thought that they could get immunity by drinking it, sniffing it, or splashing it on the body. Despite the fact that it had long been proven not to confer any immunity, the Vinegar of Four Thieves was used as late as 1793 when yellow fever hit Philadelphia.

THE WORLD IN A COUPLE OF SHAKES

As explorers began to travel the world's seas, vinegar became a vital ingredient of food preservation, and it's likely that the New Worlds would not have been discovered quite as quickly without it.

COMMERCIAL BREAK

The Industrial Revolution started a change in the commercial production of vinegar. The distillation of wood was used to produce acetic acid (the main ingredient of vinegar). After dilution and colouring with caramel or burnt sugar it was sold to an unsuspecting public as the real thing.

PASTEUR'S PUBLICATION

Despite the most far fetched theories proferred to explain the process of successful alcohol production, everyone agreed that a certain temperature and air were fundamental ingredients. But nobody discovered the reason for the formation of a veil on the surface of wine until Louis Pasteur published the most modern scientific research on vinegar, still used as a reference today. It was in 1865 that Pasteur solved the mystery surrounding vinegar. He had been asked to identify methods of keeping wine and vinegar, both commodities of great importance in France, in top condition, without deterioration during production, storage and transport. His work and treatment method became known as Pasteurization, and were later applied to milk. (You can read more about this in the Science section.)

It was this research that brought about the process for commercial production of vinegar.

VICTORIAN CONTRACEPTIVES

Vinegar was also used as a cheap yet somewhat unreliable contraceptive by the prostitutes of Victorian times.

The Science of Vinegar Production

The earliest method of making vinegar was to leave wine or beer in an open container and wait for it to turn sour. The French word *vinaigre* means sour wine. The word *alegar* was also used at one time to denote vinegar made from beer or ale.

THE ORLEANS METHOD
The French developed a more sophisticated way for producing quality vinegar, a product which has always been important, thanks to its contribution to the wine industry. Their method was to leave wine in wooden casks for two to six months until it slowly turned into vinegar. This was then filtered into other casks and left to mature for a period of months or years. The technique became known as the Orleans method, after the place where it was perfected. Good quality wines were used to make good quality vinegar, and the practice continues today, giving fine vinegars the character and subtlety that make them distinct.

LET IT LIE
As with red and white wines, red wine vinegar is left to mature for a longer time than white wine vinegar. Vinegars made by the slow Orleans method are as complex and full of flavour as fine wines and can be just as expensive.

MOTHER KNOWS BEST
The vinegar generator used in this method is a large, wooden barrel laid on its side with the bung hole facing upwards. In each end of the barrel a hole is drilled about three-quarters of the way up, so that when the liquid in the barrel is just below these holes, the barrel will be about three-quarters full. The barrel is then filled to this point with beer or diluted wine and a starter of untreated vinegar still containing active 'mother', (another name for the vinegar bacteria). The holes in the ends are covered with a fine mesh, or loose cloth, to keep out insects, and the generator is left to sit for several months. The optimum temperature for this conversion is about 29°C (84°F).

ROLL OUT THE BARREL

After this resting time the alcohol has been almost entirely converted to vinegar and it is drawn off through a spiggot placed near the bottom of the barrel on one end, leaving about 15 per cent. behind to charge the next batch, which would be added through the bung hole using a long funnel reaching below the surface level of the charging vinegar. The reason for the latter is that a scum forms on the surface of the mash as it is converted to vinegar. This is a very active layer of acetobacter and it forms on the surface, because that is precisely where there is most oxygen. While succeeding batches of vinegar will process even if this layer is broken up, they will get off to a much better start if the layer remains undisturbed.

TALKING ABOUT MY GENERATION

In the early 18th century a Dutch technologist, Hermann Boerhaave, discovered that the rate of acid production is directly related to the amount of surface exposed to air, so more air was introduced into the casks. Vinegar generators grew in size, thus increasing the distance which the mash would travel over the porous materials, thereby increasing the oxygen that reaches the mash as well. The latest of the advances, continuous aeration, (made as recently as 1952) is the use of submerged fermentation which consists of aerating the entire mash with tiny bubbles, much as an aquarium aerator works when attached to a pummace tip and placed at the bottom of the generator. This method introduces oxygen to the entire volume of the mash at all times and can reduce the time necessary for conversion from several months, to several days.

GO WITH THE FLOW

CHEMICAL FORMULA

SUGARS
(grape, beetroot/beet, apple juice...)

ALCOHOLS FERMENTATION
(biological agents: yeast)

ALCOHOLS
(wine, beetroot/beet juice, cider...)

ACETIC FERMENTATION
(biological agents: acetobacters)

$C_2H_3OH + O^2 - CH_3COOH + H^2O$

Alcohol + oxygen — acetic acid + water

VINEGARS
(wine vinegar, spirit vinegar, cider vinegar...)

PASTEUR'S DISCOVERY

Pasteur's research on fermentation and the role of microscopic organisms allowed him to uncover the process of acetification, or acidification, produced by bacteria. The acetobacter, all of 1000th of a millimeter, is transported through dust in the air. He named it mycoderma aceti because he believed that it was a fungus. These bacteria fix the oxygen in the air to the alcohol and change it into an acid. Gradually, during the fermentation process, the bacteria develop on the surface to form a whitish veil or skin, called the 'mother' of the vinegar. Mother is actually cellulose, (a natural carbohydrate which is the fibre in foods like celery and lettuce) produced by the harmless vinegar bacteria. When this skin of bacteria accumulates to a certain point, the bacteria die and fall to the bottom of the container. This continues until all the alcohol in it is exhausted.

Today, most manufacturers pasteurize their product before bottling, to prevent these bacteria from forming mother while sitting on the grocery store shelf.

FERMENTATION

Through the centuries vinegar has been produced from many other materials including molasses, sorghum, fruits, berries, melons, coconut, honey, beer, maple syrup, potatoes, beets, malt, grains and whey. But the principle remains unchanged — fermentation of natural sugars to alcohol and then secondary fermentation to vinegar. Wine, beer or any liquid containing less than 18% alcohol becomes vinegar when acetobacter aceti converts the alcohol into acetic acid.

SWEET OR SOUR?

Malt vinegar is made by the two-fold fermentation of barley malt or other cereals, where starch has been converted to maltose.

Sugar vinegars are made by the two-fold fermentation of solutions of sugar syrup or molasses. Vinegar can be made from any fruit, or from any material containing sugar. Varieties of vinegar are classified according to material from which they are made and method of manufacturing. Apple juice is most commonly used, but other notable fruits, such as grapes, peaches and berries are also popular. Labels describe starting materials, such as 'apple cider vinegar,' or 'wine vinegar' or 'rice wine vinegar.' Spirit or distilled vinegar is made by the acetic fermentation of dilute distilled alcohol.

COMMERCIALLY PRODUCED VINEGARS

More modern methods of production are designed to allow more oxygen to reach the acetobacter. The first of these methods was to use a larger vat loosely packed with a porous material, such as pommace (grape pulp, after pressing), or beechwood shavings. The mash was allowed to slowly trickle down on to these materials, thus greatly increasing the amount of surface area for the volume of mash. This allowed for much more rapid production of vinegar with better controls. Further improvements came with the addition of more holes in the generator, allowing for freer passage of air through the vat and the oxygen which it brought. As the wine trickles down it takes on some of the flavour of the wood and the airborne acetobacter uses oxygen in the air around the loosely packed wood-chips to oxidize the alcohol in the wine, turning it into acetic acid. The quality of vinegars produced by this method varies according to the quality of the wine used. It is these 'lost' elements of the wine that develop in the cask using the Orleans method.

ACETIC ACID CONTENT
The acetic acid content, often referred to as the 'sourness' of vinegars, varies according to what they are made from. Rice vinegars are the mildest and distilled vinegar is the strongest. Beer and wine vinegars generally fall in the middle of the range, with wine vinegars slightly more acetic than those made from beer or cider.

ALTERNATIVE VINEGARS
Vinegars made from other alcoholic liquids are made in much the same way as wine vinegar. The better quality ones are also stored and matured in wood. These other types can be made from fruit juices, syrups, like honey and molasses, and cane sugar.

INDUSTRIAL VINEGAR
There are also cheap (and nasty) vinegars made from ethyl alcohol, a by-product of the pulp and paper industry, and from diluted artificial acetic acid. These are definitely not for the discerning palate!

In the late 1800s chemists learned to make acetic acid. Manufacturers added water, to reduce its strength to 5%, and colouring, and sold it as vinegar. Imitation vinegar is still manufactured and by law the label must state that it is diluted acetic acid. Diluted acetic acid is inexpensive but lacks the vitamins and minerals found in fermented vinegar. The flavour and aroma are also inferior.

WILD YEAST
It takes good quality alcohol to make fermented vinegar. The hit-or-miss method of making vinegar by allowing sugar and water to ferment is not ill-advised. The fermentation of sugar to alcohol by wild yeast is followed by a conversion of the alcohol to acetic acid by wild bacteria. The chances of failure or undesirable tastes and aromas are

therefore high. If you make your own vinegar, control the process by using great care in cleanliness and introducing chosen yeast and bacteria to obtain quality vinegar every time.

HOME BREWING
If you attempt to make vinegar at home, you'll soon develop an appreciation for the difficulty of this ancient art. Be cautious: while home-made vinegar can be good for dressing salads and general purpose usage, the acidity may not be adequate for safe use in pickling and canning. Unless you are certain the acidity is at least 4%, avoid pickling or canning with it.

The acetobacter reaction, unlike that of yeast on sugar to make alcohol, is an aerobic reaction. It requires the presence of oxygen. The more oxygen, the better. Most of the improvements in vinegar production have emerged from identification of better ways to get greater amounts of oxygen to the bacteria in a shorter period of time. The next necessity is to keep insects away from the acetifying must while allowing for the air flow.

VINEGAR IS COOL!
Because of its acid nature, vinegar is self-preserving and does not need refrigeration. White vinegar will remain virtually unchanged over an extended period of time. While some changes can be observed in other types of vinegars, such as colour changes or the development of a haze or sediment, this does not harm the product, which can still be used with confidence.

GERMAN ALCHEMY
A 16th century alchemist synthesized acetic acid from inorganic materials for the first time.

VINEGAR PAPER
Used to make cellulose, it is a by-product of the vinegar making process.

SCIENTIFIC USES OF VINEGAR PAPER:
Produces pigments useful for art
Oil spill clean-up sponge
Absorptive base for toxic material removal
Petroleum and mining
Mineral and oil recovery
Clothing and shoes
Artificial leather products
One-piece textiles
Outdoor sports
Disposable tents and camping gear
Water purification via ultra filters and reverse osmosis membranes
Audio products
Superior audio speaker diaphragms
Forest products
Artificial wood strengthener (plywood laminates)
Filler for paper
High strength containers
Speciality papers
Archival document repair
Paper base for long-lived currency
Automotive and aircraft
Car bodies
Airplane structural elements
Rocket casings for deep space missions
Binder in papers
Artificial arteries/vessels/skin

Conversion Charts for Measures

The recipes and tips included in this book come from a variety of sources. Some of the old recipes are given in their original, imperial state. Where possible, these have been converted to metric equivalents. Others use the American cup, so I have included the conversion charts to assist. All food is now sold in metric units, so it makes sense to measure ingredients that way wherever possible.

There are, however, a few things to remember when following instructions.

If a recipe only lists imperial quantities, it's better to use your old imperial weights rather than try to convert it all.

Don't switch between imperial and metric within one recipe. There will be small discrepancies between equivalent weights, so you could end up with the wrong proportions of ingredients.

On tall, narrow measuring jugs, there's a greater distance between the calibrations on the side, so it's easier to judge differences in small quantities.

Spoon measurements convert easily to millilitres, and vice versa.

$^{1}/_{2}$ tsp	2.5 ml	2 tbsp	30 ml
1 tsp	5 ml	3 tbsp	45 ml
$1^{1}/_{2}$ tsp	7.5 ml	4 tbsp	60 ml
2 tsp	10 ml	5 tbsp	75 ml
1 tbsp	15 ml	6 tbsp	90 ml

GRAMS TO OUNCES

10 g	0.25 oz	225 g	8 oz
15 g	0.38 oz	250 g	9 oz
25 g	1 oz	275 g	10 oz
50 g	2 oz	300 g	11 oz
75 g	3 oz	350 g	12 oz
110 g	4 oz	375 g	13 oz
150 g	5 oz	400 g	14 oz
175 g	6 oz	425 g	15 oz
200 g	7 oz	450 g	15 oz

METRIC TO CUPS

Description	Metric	Cups
Flour etc	115 g	1 cup
Golden syrup, treacle (molasses), clear honey	350 g	1 cup
Liquids	225 ml	1 cup

LIQUID MEASURES

fl oz	pints	ml
5 fl oz	$^1/_4$ pt	150 ml
7.5 fl oz		215 ml
10 fl oz	$^1/_2$ pt	275 ml
15 fl oz		425 ml
20 fl oz	1 pt	570 ml
35 fl oz	$1^3/_4$ pt	1 litre

TEMPERATURE

Celsius	Fahrenheit	Gas mark	Description
110°C	225°F	$1/4$	very cool
130°C	250°F	$1/2$	very cool
140°C	275°F	1	cool
150°C	300°F	2	cool
170°C	325°F	3	very moderate
180°C	350°F	4	moderate
190°C	375°F	5	moderate
200°C	400°F	6	moderately hot
220°C	425°F	7	hot
230°C	450°F	8	hot
240°C	475°F	9	very hot

Main Types
of Vinegar

MALT VINEGAR

Malt results when grain is softened by steeping in water and allowing germination. Germination causes the natural enzymes in the grain to become active and help digest the starch present in the grain. The starch is converted into sugars prior to fermentation. Malt has a distinctive taste that contributes to the flavour of malt vinegar and brewed beverages such as beer.

Malt vinegar is the most commonly used variety in Britain and northern Europe, ie the beer drinking countries of Europe. It is made from soured, unhopped beer and may be coloured with caramel to give it a familiar brown colour. Malt vinegar can be flavoured with black and white peppercorns, allspice, cloves or tiny hot chillies. It is often sold as pickling vinegar; for pickling onions, walnuts and for making piccalilli. The acetic content is around 4%. Any English recipe calling for vinegar usually uses malt vinegar, unless otherwise noted.

Distilled malt is good with watery vegetables. Some people swear by vinegar on cabbage to bring out the flavour, but maybe that's an acquired taste.

Distilled malt vinegar is a must with chips (French fries), though, and however much our French friends have ridiculed my family in the past, we have converted some with the explanation that vinegar emulsifies the fat on the chips and prevents the body from absorbing excess fat.

White distilled vinegar is a cheap product that is used for mundane jobs, like cleaning glass, coffee pots, and as a detergent or disinfectant. Distilled from ethyl alcohol, it's a bit too harsh for most recipes, except pickling. (This may discolour light-coloured fruits and vegetables.)

SPIRIT VINEGAR
This vinegar is distilled before the acetification process has finished and contains a small amount of alcohol which changes the flavour dimension. This is the strongest of all the vinegars and is used for the same purposes as distilled vinegar.

WINE VINEGAR
This is the strongest natural vinegar, with an acidity of 6.5%. It can be flavoured with herbs, honey, spices flower petals or seaweed. Wine vinegar comes as red or white, and the best are produced by the Orleans method (see The Science of Vinegar Production). Slow fermentation in oak casks for up to two years produces a depth of flavour, but high acidity. Red wine vinegars are aged longer than those made from white wine. The very best wine vinegars are made in relatively small batches, have fine balance and subtle, complex flavours. They are characteristically rich and mellow.

Commercially produced wine vinegars are of an inferior quality, using average wine and faster production techniques that remove a lot of the more subtle flavours in the wine. Many commercially produced wines are, however, very good, and as with so many things, the price reflects the quality.

RED WINE VINEGARS
Cabernet Sauvignon wine vinegar
Produced from fermentation of Cabernet Sauvignon wine. It is of high quality and a rich burgundy colour.

Merlot wine vinegar
This is one of the best. It has a unique flavour and aroma and is dark red in colour.

Pinot Noir wine vinegar
Clear, bright and medium red in colour, this vinegar
has unique characteristics

Raspberry red wine vinegar
Natural raspberry flavour is added to red wine
vinegar which is the aged and filtered product
obtained from the acetous fermentation of select
red wine. Raspberry Red Wine Vinegar has a
characteristic dark red colour and a piquant, yet
delicate raspberry flavour. Uses: Sprinkle raspberry
vinegar on fruit salads; use as a marinade or basting
sauce for meats; use as an ingredient in your
favourite salad dressing, or use by itself on salads
or cooked vegetables.

WHITE WINE VINEGAR
This is a moderately tangy vinegar that French
cooks use to make Hollandaise and Béarnaise
sauces, vinaigrettes, soups and stews.

White wine vinegar is the aged and filtered product
obtained through the acetous fermentation of a
selected blend of white wines. It is clear and pale
gold, almost colourless. The taste is distinctly
acidic, and the aroma reminiscent of the wine from
which it comes. White wine vinegar can be used to
bring out the sweetness in strawberries and melons.
Adding a twist to spicy salsas and marinades can
wake up the flavour of sauces and glazes. This
product is perfect for today's lighter cooking style
— replace heavy cream or butter with a splash of
white wine vinegar to balance flavours without
adding fat. The tart, tangy taste also reduces the
need for salt.

Chardonnay wine vinegar
This has a distinctive flavour and aroma, and is light
to medium gold in colour.

Zinfandel wine vinegar
This is a clear, bright, transparent product as the result of Zinfandel wine acetous fermentation.

CHAMPAGNE VINEGAR
As to be expected, this vinegar is expensive, delicate, refined and gentle. Its pale gold colour is clear and bright, although you wouldn't want to drink a glass of it. This light and mild vinegar is a good choice if you want to dress delicately flavoured salads or vegetables. Mix it with nut or truffle oil to make a sublime vinaigrette.

CIDER VINEGAR
In the manufacture of cider vinegar the pure apple juice is fermented into cider, exposed to air so that it sours and is converted to acetic acid. The result is a clear, pale honey brown, vinegar although unpasteurized versions can be cloudy, with a strong apple taste. It is best for pickling pears or plums spiced with cloves and cinnamon and can be sweetened with dark sugar. Cider vinegar may darken light-coloured fruits and vegetables.

Many people, especially it seems in the USA, advocate the use of cider vinegar, especially organic varieties, as a health promoting beverage Good quality cider vinegar can be diluted for medicinal uses.

(See the section on Uses for Health & Personal Care.)

It is milder and less acidic than wine vinegar and good for salad dressing where the salad contains fruit.

HERB VINEGARS

Steep bunches of fresh herbs in bottles of wine vinegar for adding subtle flavours to dressings. Rice or cider vinegars may be substituted as good bases for most herb vinegars.

Tarragon is one of the most popular and is especially good on eggs, as well as being an essential ingredient in Sauce Béarnaise. Just put one or two sprigs of clean, fresh tarragon in a bottle of warm white wine vinegar, tightly seal the bottle, and let it stand for a few days.

You may also like to try thyme, rosemary basil, garlic or green peppercorns in red wine vinegar.

RICE VINEGARS

Rice vinegars are made from soured and fermented rice wines. Those from China are stronger, being sharp and sour. Chinese rice wines tend to be clear, although some are shades of red and brown.

Japanese rice vinegars tend to be softer, mellower and sweetish. They are mostly clear or straw-coloured.There are two distinct types of Japanese vinegar; one is made from fermented rice and the other is made by adding rice vinegar to sake.

Rice vinegar is excellent for flavouring with herbs, spices and fruits. Widely used in Asian dishes, rice vinegar is popular because it does not significantly alter the appearance of the food.

Rice vinegar is one of the keys to good oriental cooking. Because of its sourness, which is able to bring out the sweetness, saltiness and 'umami' (glutamate-like taste) it deepens the taste of the entire dish. The aroma of vinegar is another important element in oriental cooking. A well-balanced, mild and aromatic vinegar is of utmost importance when putting together cooking materials to make delicious, aromatic dishes.

Chencu, or mature vinegar, which has been used as a kind of flavouring for more than 1,000 years in China, is being used for other purposes by modern Chinese people, who are advocating a healthy lifestyle. Chencu is a liquid with a delicate fragrance and dark colour. Scientific research shows that the vinegar contains 18 amino acids such as enzymes and lactic acid, and 17 kinds of trace elements such as calcium, iron, zinc and manganese, needed by the human body. The content of the acetic acid in Chencu is the highest among all vinegar products.

In Japan improvements through the centuries came with chefs who had the knack for recipe variation. The 17th century saw delicate finger foods complemented with vinegar. Matsumoto Yoshiichi of Edo (Tokyo) introduced the use of rice vinegar into sushi rice. The vinegar was a welcome ingredient, reducing the usual lengthy preparation while adding a pleasant flavour of tartness.

White rice vinegar

This Asian vinegar is milder and sweeter than Western vinegars. It's used in Japan to make sushi, rice and salads, and in China to flavour stir-fries, particularly sweet and sour dishes, for soups and for pickling.

Western cooks often use it to flavour delicate chicken or fish dishes, or to dress salads or vegetables. Japanese brands tend to be milder than Chinese, but they can be interchanged.

This is a colourless liquid, higher in vinegar content and more similar in flavour to distilled vinegars. The sweetness comes from the glutinous rice.

Black rice vinegar

Black rice vinegar is very popular in southern China in the province of Chinkiang vinegar is made. Normally black rice vinegar is made with glutinous or sweet rice, although millet or sorghum may be used instead. More assertive than white rice vinegar, and dark in colour, it has a deep, almost smoky flavour. Black rice vinegar works well in braised dishes and as a dipping sauce. It can also serve as a substitute for balsamic vinegar.

Red rice vinegar

This is another vinegar that is dark in colour, but lighter than black rice vinegar. Red rice vinegar is an intriguing combination of salty or tart, and sweet. It can be used as a substitute for black vinegar — just add a bit of sugar. It makes a very good dipping sauce, and you can also use it in noodles, soup and seafood dishes (you'll often find it in recipes for Hot and Sour and Shark's Fin Soup).

Seasoned rice vinegar

Accomplished Asian cooks who find this in your pantry are likely to purse their lips, just as Italian cooks would over a packet of spaghetti sauce mix. It's lightly flavoured with sugar and salt, and saves time when making sushi. You can also use it to dress salads, vegetables and other dishes.

SHERRY VINEGAR

Sherry vinegar is Spain's answer to balsamic vinegar. Some consider sherry vinegar the 'king of all vinegars'. In fact, good quality sherry vinegar costs much more than sherry itself.

Sherry vinegar was always produced by accident, or by poor wine making practices. Winemakers gave the vinegar to their families or friends for cooking. They were ashamed to admit that some of their wines had too much volatile acidity and was thus unfit for sherry.

Vinegar from sherry grape must, or newly pressed juice has a rich, nutty, sweet flavour. Although quite different from balsamic, it is good to sprinkle over salads or cooked vegetables on its own. As with other wine vinegars, the best ones are very expensive. Sherry vinegars are made from a blend of wines, just like sherry, and are left to mature in the wood for a long time. Barrels containing too much volatile acidity are never used for sherry or brandy. The vinegar must be aged in the wood for at least two years, and some companies age their vinegars for 20 to 30 years, hence the king's ransom! They develop rich flavour and a mellow complexity. Assertive yet smooth, they are great for deglazing pans and perking up sauces, especially those that will accompany hearty meats like duck, beef or game.

BALSAMIC VINEGAR
This is the vinegar made only in or around Modena in Northern Italy. Balsam means balm.

The very finest Balsamics are made from the juice of Trebbiano white and sugary grapes that has been concentrated down, over a low flame, almost to a syrup. Custom demands that the grapes are harvested as late as possible to take advantage of the warmth that nature provides there. This vinegar is then filtered into wooden casks and left to mature for anywhere from 10 to 30 years, some for even longer. There are reports of 11th century producers maturing this product for over 100 years, and giving over vast areas of their estates to producing enough for family culinary use. Those who can afford them use them in desserts, where their sweetness and subtleties can be shown off to best advantage and the ladies of Modena take their older balsamico in traditional style, straight from the glass as a digestif as they would a vintage port, after having dined too well on veal with cream, while their menfolk consider it an aid to virility.

There was a time when aged balsamics were never sold but could only be acquired as gifts: a bride's worth was assessed on how many barrels came with her dowry.

Some Balsamics mature in a succession of casks all made from a different type of wood, such as oak, cherrywood, ash, mulberry and juniper, which contribute to its taste, each type giving another layer of flavour to the vinegar. It is this almost magical combination of wood, wine and time that makes traditionally made Balsamic vinegar such a rare and expensive delight.

Fermenting very slowly in barrels and blending over a period of eight to twelve years produces a unique dark, almost treacly, sweet–and-sour amber liquid, making an excellent salad dressing. Sauces and gravies benefit from the addition of balsamic vinegar. Sprinkle on cooked meats to add flavour and aroma, or season salad greens, strawberries, peaches and melons. The vinegar-makers of Modena recommend their younger brews of 8–10 years for salads and adding to gravies, while the older vinegars – the 15–20-year-olds or more – are best with shavings of Parmesan, or as a dressing for gravadlax or tuna carpaccio.

Commercially made Balsamic vinegar is made in the region as well, and while nowhere near the quality of the traditionally made vinegar, it is very good and markedly different from other wine vinegars. Balsamic vinegar made in the traditional way is an outstanding vinegar, but one which is very labour intensive and time consuming. Therefore, it is very expensive and available in limited quantities.

FRUIT VINEGAR

In Victorian times fruit vinegars were used as a basis for refreshing drinks, for cooking duck, roasting ham and in other fatty or rich meats.

Fruit vinegar is often made from raspberries, blueberries, blackberries, cranberries or mango. The resulting products tend to be sweet and delicate in flavour and aroma and make a nice complement to fruits and many salads, or they can be used in salad dressings, such as raspberry vinaigrette. They are a healthy alternative to more robust vinegars, and since they're not as pungent as other vinegars, you can cut calories by using less oil. They're also good in marinades and in sauces for roasted meats, especially poultry, ham, pork and veal.

They're easy enough to make at home, but use a trustworthy recipe. If too much fruit is added to the vinegar, it may not be sufficiently acidic to ward off harmful microbes.

Pineapple vinegar is used in Mexico, but difficult to find elsewhere. It's reputedly good, although you could substitute cider vinegar.

UMEBOSHI VINEGAR

This Japanese vinegar is a pink brine, and it has a deep cherry aroma and a fruity, sour flavour. It is a by-product produced when umeboshi (Japanese pickled plums) is made. Technically, it is not classified as a vinegar because it contains salt, but is a good substitute for vinegar and salt in any recipe. It has a light, citric flavour and is typically used in dips and salad dressings and adding flavour to steamed vegetables.

It's interesting to note that drinking vinegar has become a national pastime in Japan over the last few years, with average monthly sales at Uchibori's six fruit vinegar stalls jumping by 10 per cent in two years. The Oak Heart stall in a department store in Tokyo stocks an impressive array of fruit vinegars, including lychee, raspberry, cranberry, mango, apple and rosehip. The most popular is blueberry and about 80 bottles are sold each day at £6.30 each (1,250 yen). New products will include plastic bottles of vinegar water sold at 24 hour convenience stores. Maybe there's something in the idea of a sour taste to relieve humidity-induced fatigue. Many Americans swear by apple cider vinegar for all sorts of ailments which cause fatigue.

CANE VINEGAR
This vinegar is most commonly used in Philippine cooking. It is made from sugarcane and has a rich, slightly sweet flavour. Cane vinegar is essential in making pickles, mustards and vinaigrettes. It adds flavour to numerous sauces, marinades and dressings, and to preparations such as sauerbraten, sweet and sour dishes and marinated herring.

COCONUT VINEGAR
Coconut vinegar is potent, low in acidity, with a musty flavour and a unique aftertaste. It is used in many Thai dishes. Coconut vinegars are common in India, the Philippines and Indonesia.

DATE VINEGAR
Date vinegar is popular in the Middle East.

CORN SUGAR VINEGAR
This results from the alcoholic and subsequent acetous fermentation of corn sugar and has a smooth, mild flavour. It has a distinctive amber colour.

In the Laundry

LAUNDRY USES

Only use white vinegar for the following tips and applications.

LABEL REMOVER
Soak the label or sticker with vinegar, leave until it is saturated, then peel off.

GETTING RID OF UNDERARM MARKS
Perspiration marks can be eliminated by soaking them with vinegar before laundering in the usual way. To remove the solid residue on the underarm of a shirt left by deodorants, soak the area in white vinegar until saturated then wash as usual. This also removes any odour as well.

COLLARS AND CUFFS
Collars and cuffs can be cleaned by rubbing a thick paste of bicarbonate of soda (baking soda) and vinegar on to the stains before washing in the usual way.

FABRIC SOFTENER AND STATIC CLING REDUCER
Use as you would a liquid fabric softener.

STAIN REMOVER
For stains caused by grass, coffee, tea, fruits and berries, soak clothing in full strength vinegar.

TERRY NAPPIES (DIAPERS) I
Use 275 ml (½ pint) of vinegar in 9 litres (2 gallons) of water in the nappy pail to neutralize the urine in cloth nappies. It also helps to keep them from staining.

TERRY NAPPIES (DIAPERS) II
Adding 275 ml (½ pint) vinegar during the rinse cycle equalizes the pH balance and has been reported to prevent nappy rash.

TERRY NAPPIES (DIAPERS) III
Using vinegar in the wash cycle cuts the cost. Use half the recommended detergent during the wash and skip the fabric softener. Instead, put the nappies through an additional rinse at the end.

CUTTING DOWN LINT ON CLOTHING
Another reason to use vinegar in the rinse cycle is that it cuts down on the lint. Put 150–275 ml (¼–½ pint) in the rinse cycle. You will notice the reduction in lint on the family's clothes.

PREVENTING COLOURS RUNNING
Use white vinegar if washing something that will bleed. Pour some white vinegar in the washer filling with cold water and then add soap and clothes.

REMOVING TAR FROM JEANS
Pour a few drops of vinegar on the stains, then put them in the washing machine and wash as normal.

REMOVING STIFFNESS FROM NEW JEANS
Wash jeans for the first time by turning them inside out and adding 275 ml (½ pint) of vinegar to the wash. It takes the stiffness out of new jeans.

REMOVING WHITE MARKS WHEN LETTING DOWN HEMS
When you let down hems on children's clothes such as skirts, dresses etc., there is often a white mark where the fabric was turned up. Warm up your iron, and with an old toothbrush dipped in a little vinegar diluted with small amount of water, scrub the mark and press. It usually comes right out. If not, then repeat.

PREVENTING FADING OF COLOURED TOWELS AND QUILTS
Add 150 ml (¼ pint) of vinegar to the laundry to prevent fading. Handmade quilts can be soaked in lots of cold water using 275 ml (½ pint) of vinegar on the first time of laundering.

DYEING
When dyeing fabric, include 275 ml (½ pint) white vinegar in a hot dye bath to set the colour.

GETTING RID OF SHINY MARKS WHEN IRONING
Mix half vinegar and half water and put into a spritzer bottle. When ironing, use the spray to help remove iron-made creases or shiny areas in the fabric. Spritz a shirt for a clean, odour-free, crisp garment, especially collars and underarm areas. Use a damp cloth and gently rub shiny areas like those that appear when the iron is too hot and you iron over a zipper, then repress and the shine will be gone. Repeat if necessary.

REMOVING OR SETTING CREASES
For setting creases and also removing them when in the wrong place, iron with a pressing cloth soaked in a solution of 1 part vinegar to 2 parts water. This is a strong, smelly solution so use in a well ventilated room. The smell will soon leave the garment after airing.

CLEANING AND REFRESHING AN IRONING BOARD
Spritz the ironing board cover to freshen it up and iron while it is still damp. This is cheaper than any purchased fabric freshener or odour eliminator.

STEAM IRON CLEANER
Mineral deposits may be removed from an old steam iron by filling it with a solution of equal parts white vinegar and water and letting it steam until dry. Rinse the tank with clean water, refill it and shake water through the steam holes over an old piece of material. Test on an old cloth before ironing. It is not advisable to try this on a new iron as the acidity of the vinegar may damage the iron.

CLEANING THE BASE OF AN IRON
Use a paste of vinegar and bicarbonate of soda (baking soda) to clean the sole plate of your iron. It will be smooth, clean and shiny and will not harm any surface.

SOFT AND FLUFFY BLANKETS
570 ml (1 pint) of white vinegar added to a tub of water will make a good rinse for both cotton and wool blankets and leaves them free of soap, with their nap as soft and fluffy as new.

REMOVING THE SMELL OF BLEACH
If you use bleach to remove stains or to whiten cotton, remove the bleach smell by adding 275 ml (½ pint) of vinegar to the final rinse.

REMOVING COLA STAINS
Remove spots caused by cola-based soft drinks from 100% cotton, and cotton polyester fabrics. Sponge distilled vinegar directly on to the stain and rub away the spots, then clean according to the directions on the manufacturer's label. This must be done within 24 hours of the spill.

REMOVING GREASE FROM SUEDE
Dip a toothbrush in vinegar and gently brush over the grease spot.

REMOVING THE SMELL OF SMOKE FROM CLOTHES
Get the stale cigarette smoke smell out of clothes by adding 275 ml (½ pint) of vinegar to a bath of hot water.

Hang the clothes above the steam. Leave them in the bathroom overnight, with a window open if possible.

DEODORIZING A WOOL SWEATER
Wash the sweater, then rinse in equal parts of vinegar and water to remove odours.

Outdoor Uses

IN THE GARDEN

GETTING RID OF SLUGS
If you have a slug problem, drop a few drops of white vinegar on them. Be careful not to get the vinegar on your plants.

LAWNS WITH NO BROWN PATCHES
Put a tablespoon of vinegar in your dog's drinking water every day and you will no longer have those brown spots in your lawn from the dog's urine. See the section on Pets & Animals for further benefits.

INSTANT ANTIBACTERIAL AID FOR GARDENERS OR RAMBLERS
If you hate to wear gloves when gardening (except, of course when working with roses, blackberries or thistles) you will, once in a while, get nicked or scratched. White vinegar can be used to treat such scratches if you are on the allotment, or miles from a water supply. This stings for a second or two, but saves a long trek to the tap.

REMOVING STAINS FROM FLOWERPOTS
That staining that occurs in clay and plastic flower pots and their saucers comes right out without scrubbing. Just fill the kitchen sink with cold water and add plain white vinegar about $\frac{2}{3}$ water to $\frac{1}{3}$ vinegar. Soak the pots and saucers until they look clean and new. This may take up to an hour. Wash with soap and water before reusing.

DISCOURAGING ANTS
If you have problems with ants and other insects invading your home, they are probably crossing your doorways and window sills. If you pour vinegar across the opening sill, it stops them from crossing.

WEED SUPPRESSANT I
Mix 3 parts water with 1 part concentrated
acetic acid, or vinegar, to get a final concentration
of 6%. You should be able to achieve a 6% acetic
acid concentration by mixing household table
vinegar with concentrated lemon or lime juice
in equal parts.

This will act on the young tender new growth of
plants. It is not taken into the roots but basically
burns the top growth. If repeated consistently
every week to 10 days during the vigorous growing
season, it will eventually kill off the plants by
starving the roots.

Please note that this is a suppressant for hardier
perennial weeds, not a weed killer.

It may be effective on young annual plants and
should help control perennials with multiple
applications.

WEED SUPPRESSANT II
Kill individual weeds by pouring hot vinegar on.
This might take a couple of times to work
completely. I would suggest this treatment for
patios and paths, rather than lawns, or amongst
precious herbaceous beds.

Alternatively, use white vinegar straight from the
bottle to pour on the weeds and grasses that come
up through the pavement. Pour on and leave for a
couple of days. The weeds will die back and won't
reappear for several months.

REPELLING MOSQUITOES
Add a tablespoon of apple cider vinegar to a quart
of drinking water. This helps to deal with heat
stress and also helps to repel mosquitoes.

RIPENING MELONS WITHOUT MOULD
Try rubbing each melon with about a teaspoonful of full-strength vinegar every few days as they begin to ripen.

KEEPING CATS OUT OF THE CHILDREN'S SAND TRAY
Pour vinegar around the children's sand box to keep cats from using it as their litter box. Reapply about every two months just to be sure.

TO INCREASE SOIL ACIDITY
In hard water areas, add a 275 ml (½ pint) of vinegar to 4.5 litres (1 gallon) of tap water for watering acid-loving plants like rhododendrons, heathers or azaleas. The vinegar will release iron in the soil for the plants to use.

Azaleas will benefit from an occasional watering with a mixture of two tablespoons of vinegar to 1 litre (1¾ pints) of water.

TO NEUTRALIZE GARDEN LIME
Rinse your hands liberally with vinegar after working with garden lime to avoid rough and flaking skin.

AROUND THE HOUSE

TO DISSOLVE CHEWING GUM
Saturate the area with vinegar. If the vinegar is heated, it will work faster.

SEPTIC TANK USERS
If you have a septic tank, use vinegar instead of harsh chemicals to clean the toilet bowl. Leave overnight if you can. It will help to keep the germs down.

KEEPING FLIES FROM A SWIMMING POOL
Pour vinegar around the sides of your pool and it helps keeps flies away.

CLEANING WINDOWS
Clean windows with a solution of two tablespoons of vinegar to 1 litre (3½ pints) of warm water. Wash from top to bottom on the inside of windows and from side to side on the outside. This way you will be able to tell on which side any smears are.

Using dry newspaper instead of a cloth to polish with is an old trick as well.

Keep a solution of 50/50 white vinegar and water in a spray bottle to use for removing spots from windows. See also Cleaning Uses & Odour Control for another recipe.

DRAIN CLEANER
Vinegar and bicarbonate of soda cause a chemical reaction when combined, so be prepared. They break down fatty acids from grease, other foods and a build-up of soap into simpler substances.

Pour 50 g (2 oz) of bicarbonate of soda (baking soda) and 150 ml (¼ pint) of vinegar into the drain. Cover if possible while the solution fizzes. Follow this with a bucketful of very hot water.

VINEGAR AS A WOOD STAIN

White vinegar can be mixed with water-based inks to make a wonderful stain for wood. The resulting finish is the colour of the ink with a silvery sheen. Simply pour vinegar into a mixing jar, add the ink until the desired colour is achieved and apply to the wood with a brush or rag. Wipe off any excess and let it dry. Since the bulk of the mixture is vinegar, wood-warpage is minimal.

REMOVING RUST FROM BOLTS, SCREWS, NAILS AND HINGES

To remove rust from bolts and other metals, soak them in full strength vinegar. Put the metal objects in a container and cover with vinegar. Seal the container and shake. Let it stand overnight. Dry the objects to prevent corrosion.

REMOVING PAINT FROM GLASS

Hot vinegar can be used to remove paint from glass. This works well around windows where you've accidentally got paint on the glass. Just heat up vinegar and use a cloth to wipe away the paint.

REMOVING CALCIUM BUILD-UP FROM BRICKWORK

To get rid of calcium build-up on brick or on limestone, use a spray bottle with half vinegar and half water, then just let it set. The solution will do all the work.

REMOVING DIESEL SMELLS

If you have the misfortune to spill diesel fuel either on clothes or yourself, you will know that the smell is horrible and refuses to go away. A little vinegar added to the washer takes most, if not all, the smell out.

REMOVING LIME DEPOSITS FROM WINDSCREEN JETS

Use full strength vinegar on a rag to wipe away the lime deposits left on your car's paint and windows.

CLEANING WINDSCREENS AND KEEPING ICE OFF

If you have to leave your car outside overnight in the winter, mix 3 parts vinegar to 1 part water and coat the windows with this solution. This vinegar and water combination will keep windscreens ice and frost-free.

CHROME POLISH

Apply full strength vinegar to a cloth to polish the chrome on your car.

AZALEAS

Pour vinegar over your azaleas to give a sheen over the leaves.

PROLONGING THE LIVES OF FLOWERS

Pour a mixture of vinegar and water over household plants and bouquets to prolong their lifespan.

KEEP CATS AWAY

Sprinkle a little vinegar on your garden paths and patios. This will keep cats away.

STAINS ON CONCRETE

Remove unsightly marks on concrete by applying vinegar directly to the stain.

GRASS KILLER

Kill weeds or unwanted grass with direct application of vinegar on to the trouble spot.

INCREASE SOIL ACIDITY

Make soil less alkaline by applying vinegar to give your soil a greater acidity.

Cleaning Uses & Odour Control

INDOOR CLEANING USES

Vinegar is well recognized as a cleaning and sanitizing agent. It is especially effective in removing inorganic soils and mineral deposits, such as hard water films. As a sanitizer, it is effective against a broad range of bacteria, yeasts and moulds, destroying or reducing these organisms to acceptable levels.

Additionally, vinegar has been found to be effective as a rinse agent in reducing levels of *E. coli* on various countertop surfaces (e.g., laminate, wood, tile, concrete, stainless steel and granite).

Vinegar has been used commercially to reduce micro-organisms in slaughterhouses and poultry plants; to reduce mineral and lime deposits in lavatory pipes; to prevent milk stone build-up in tanks used by the milk industry; to clean vehicles and equipment used in the construction industry and to wash and rinse walls and ceilings in restaurants and food establishments.

Cleaning with vinegar is much safer and cheaper than using commercial products and has the following additional advantages:

- It's biodegradable — a mild organic acid.
- It's easy to dispense and control.
- It's safe for stainless steel, used by the food industry.
- It's relatively nontoxic and stable, so safe for handling.
- It's less likely to leave harmful residues behind.
- It has a pleasant, clean smell.
- It can be used where environmental considerations are especially important.

Once again, Mrs Beeton and her contemporaries give insight into the many uses and applications which were known to our grandparents and great-grandparents.

NOTE: Red wine and cider vinegar should be avoided because their colouring may cause staining. White distilled vinegar is best for cleaning.

IN THE KITCHEN

REMOVING COFFEE AND TEA STAINS
An equal mixture of salt and white vinegar will clean coffee and tea stains from china cups.

LOOSENING TOUGH STAINS
To loosen hard-to-clean stains in glass or porcelain pots or pans, boil 45 ml (3 tbsp) of white vinegar with 570 ml (1 pint) of water. Wash in hot, soapy water.

BRIGHTER STAINLESS STEEL
Spots on your stainless steel or aluminium kitchen equipment can be removed by rubbing with white vinegar.

NOTE: Do not leave in vinegar, as the pots will corrode.

SOAKING BADLY STAINED POTS AND PANS
Soak non-aluminium, food-stained pots and pans in full strength white vinegar for 30 minutes. Rinse in hot, soapy water.

REMOVING FRUIT STAINS
To remove fruit stains from your hands, rub them with a little white vinegar and wipe with a cloth.

OVEN CLEANER I
Dampen your cleaning cloth in white vinegar and water and use it to wipe out your oven.

OVEN CLEANER II
To keep your freshly cleaned oven from stinking up your house next time you bake something, wipe it with white vinegar poured directly on the sponge as a final rinse. It neutralizes the harsh alkali of oven cleaners.

CLEANING KETTLES
If you get lime deposits in your kettle, gently boil 150 ml (¼ pint) of white vinegar with the water, then rinse well.

RINSING DISHES
Use white vinegar mixed with water to rinse off the dishes after washing. This will take the soap off and leave them squeaky clean. A splash of vinegar added to rinse water will also keep glasses from water spotting.

RINSING IN THE DISHWASHER
Pour 45 ml (3 tbsp) vinegar into your dishwasher rinse cycle for streak-free, sparkling dishes every time instead of using rinse aid.

MICROWAVE CLEANER
To clean a microwave oven all you need to do is put a couple of tablespoons of vinegar in a bowl with a cup of water. Microwave on high for 45 seconds to 1 minute (the time depends on your particular model). Carefully take the bowl out and wipe out the oven. Any baked-on splatters will be softened and easily removed.

REVIVING OLD KITCHEN CLOTHS:
Renew old sponges by washing them in vinegar water, then soaking overnight in a litre (1¾ pints) of water with 45 ml (3 tbsp) vinegar added to it.

CLEANING WASTE-DISPOSAL UNITS
Clean and freshen the waste-disposal unit by running a tray of ice cubes through it with 90 ml (6 tbsp) of vinegar poured over them, once a week.

CLEANING CHOPPING BOARDS
Wipe down cutting boards with full strength vinegar. It will clean them, cut grease and absorb odours.

CLEANING WORK SURFACES
Wipe all kitchen work surfaces down with full strength white vinegar to clean them and reduce bacteria.

CLEANING OUT A COFFEE MAKER
Fill the water reservoir half way with vinegar and run the coffee maker as you normally do, and then run it once full of water. The coffee maker will be spotless.

GREASE CUTTER
Vinegar is an excellent grease cutter. Boil out fat fryers every week with vinegar and water. This is very cost effective and safe, with no harsh chemicals, or risk of fire. It works well on grill hoods too.

CLEANING DECANTERS AND BOTTLES
Use a dessertspoon full of salt, moistened with vinegar. Shake well and rinse thoroughly with water.

CLEANING THE REFRIGERATOR
Clean the refrigerator by washing with a solution of equal parts of water and vinegar.

REFRESHING THE ICE TRAY
Boil some vinegar and let it cool for a while. Pour it, still hot, into the tray. Wait a few moments and then wipe it clean.

SWEET-SMELLING BREAD BOX
After cleaning out the bread box or crock, keep it smelling sweet by wiping it down with a cloth moistened in distilled vinegar. Allow to dry before replacing the bread.

CLEANING SOLUTIONS

Vinegar cleans by cutting grease. This makes it useful for melting away gummy build-up. It also inhibits mould growth, dissolves mineral accumulations, freshens the air, kills bacteria and slows its regrowth.

CHEAP CLEANING SOLUTION
1/3 part white vinegar
1/3 part rubbing alcohol (or surgical spirit)
1/3 part water
3 drops dishwashing liquid

Mix this into a (recycled) spray bottle and you have the equivalent of the floor cleaner. Just spray and mop. It is also recommended for deodorizing a room and for a fast clean-up. Use this on any tile floors with great results. The alcohol is added to make it dry faster, so you could leave it out, if you wish.

ALL-PURPOSE WINDOW WASH
45 ml (3 tbsp) white distilled vinegar
1/2 tsp liquid soap or detergent
575 ml (1 pint) water

Combine the ingredients in a spray bottle, and shake to blend. Spray it on, and then remove with a squeegee or paper towel. Polish with dry newspaper when dry. The shelf life of this mix is indefinite, but make sure you keep it in a labelled bottle.

FLOOR CLEANER WITH FRAGRANT HERBS
30 cl (2 tbsp) liquid soap or detergent
60–120 ml (4–8 tbsp) white distilled vinegar
90 ml (6 tbsp) fragrant herb tea (peppermint
    adds antibacterial qualities)

Combine ingredients in a bucket of water. Swirl the water around until it lathers a little. Proceed as normal. Discard the remainder after use.

A CLEANING FLUID FOR COPPER AND BRASS
Make a brass and copper cleaner by combining equal parts of lemon juice and vinegar. Wipe it on a paper towel and then polish with a soft, dry cloth.

CLEANING METAL SCREENS AND ALUMINIUM FURNITURE
Use vinegar to clean away mineral build-up on metal. Add 45 ml (3 tbsp) to 1 litre (1³⁄₄ pints) of water for cleaning metal screens and aluminium furniture.

CLEANING DRAINS
Keep your drains clean and working properly with vinegar. When they seem to be getting a bit sluggish, or even blocked, pour white vinegar down the kitchen and bathroom sinks and shower drain.

TARNISHED COPPER
Heavily tarnished copper or copper-alloy to be cleaned up, use a paste made of salt and vinegar.

FLOOR CLEANER
Add 150 ml (¹⁄₄ pint) vinegar to 4.5 litres (1 gallon) of water to keep your vinyl floors clean and shining.

VINYL FLOOR CLEANING
For effortless cleaning and less bending, try squirting vinegar on the head of a moistened mop and wiping over the floor. Environmentally friendly and cheap!

CARPET SPOT AND STAIN REMOVER
As a carpet spot and stain remover, take a trigger spray bottle and fill with one part white vinegar to seven parts water. Take a second spray bottle and fill with one part white, non-sudsy ammonia and seven parts water. Saturate the stain with vinegar solution. Let it soak in for a few minutes and then spray on the ammonia solution and blot thoroughly with an old towel. Repeat until the stain has gone.

REMOVING WATER STAINS FROM LEATHER
Remove water stains from leather by rubbing with a cloth dipped in a vinegar and water solution.

REVIVING LEATHER UPHOLSTERY
Leather can be revived by wiping with a damp cloth sprinkled with a little white vinegar.

CLEANING A WHIRLPOOL TUB
Pour 4.5 litres (1 gallon) of white vinegar into the water of a whirlpool tub, once a year and run it. This will keep the jets from clogging up from soap scum, etc.

CLEANING FIREPLACE DOORS
Put vinegar on newspaper and use to wipe down the insides of glass fireplace doors. Cleans instantly and does not streak.

TOILET CLEANER
Remove stubborn stains from the toilet by spraying them with vinegar and brushing vigorously. Deodorize the bowl by adding 570 ml (1 pint) of distilled vinegar. Allow it to remain for half an hour before flushing.

CLEANING A SHOWER HEAD
Clean a shower head by unscrewing it to remove the rubber washer. Place the head in a pot filled with equal parts vinegar and water, bring to a boil, then simmer for five minutes.

Alternatively, soak the shower head in vinegar overnight, then rinse in hot water, to keep it flowing freely.

REMOVING LIME DEPOSITS
Use one part vinegar to one part water to clean tiles and grouting. On newer tiles, test in an inconspicuous area first, especially if coloured grouting has been used.

CLEANING PORCELAIN ENAMEL, BATHS, SINKS AND FITTINGS
Use a half and half solution of vinegar and water.

HARD WATER DEPOSITS
Use vinegar to get rid of the hard water deposits around your sink. Soak paper towels with vinegar and place them around the area that needs to be cleaned. For cleaning the tap (faucet), you can soak the towel and wrap it around and then rubber band it in place. Do this overnight and the next morning it's easy to wipe clean. This is safe for brass taps as well.

FURNITURE POLISH
Make a furniture polish using equal parts of white vinegar and vegetable oil. Wipe it on and buff with a soft cloth.

BRASSWARE
To clean brassware without scrubbing, soak in 1 to 10 parts of white vinegar to water. To clean brass lamps, unscrew the sections and soak in bucket. All the green and black tarnish comes off in no time.

REMOVING RUST FROM CAST IRON
Make a solution of white vinegar solution; 2 parts vinegar to 1 part water, to clean the rust off cast iron pans. Soak the pan overnight in the vinegar solution and the vinegar just dissolves the rust. Very rusty pans may take an extra evening. Don't leave a pan in there too long, or you will not have a pan! The vinegar dissolves the metal.

ANTIQUE APPLIANCES
For cleaning antique appliances: Pour white vinegar straight out of the bottle on to a sponge, to soak stubborn build-up for a few minutes. After your appliance's first-time cleaning, future quick clean-ups are easiest using a small spray/squirt bottle with diluted vinegar-water.

CLEANING PHOTOCOPIER GLASS
Keep a solution of one to two tablespoons of vinegar and water in a small spray bottle for cleaning glass screens.

CLEANING PLASTIC SHOWER CURTAINS
To prevent mildew on plastic shower curtains, keep a spray bottle of vinegar and water in the bathroom and use regularly.

BRIGHTENING CARPET COLOURS
The colours in carpets and rugs will often take on a new lease of life if they are brushed with a mixture of 275 ml (½ pint) of vinegar in 4.5 litres (1 gallon) of water.

CARPET CLEANING
Use distilled vinegar to rinse your carpets after shampooing. The carpet will stay fresh longer and it removes any detergent residue. Use 60 ml (4 tbsp) per 4.5 litres (1 gallon) of water.

REMOVING NON-OILY STAINS FROM CARPETS
Apply a mixture of a teaspoon of liquid detergent and a teaspoon of distilled vinegar in 570 ml (1 pint) of lukewarm water to the stain. Rub gently with a soft brush or towel. Rinse with a towel, moistened with clean water and blot dry. Repeat until the stain is gone and then dry quickly, using a fan or hair dryer. This should be done as soon as the stain is discovered.

CLEANING PLASTICS
Plastic can be cleaned and made anti-static by wiping down with a solution of one tablespoon of distilled vinegar to 2 litres (3½ pints) of water. This should prevent dust from settling as well.

AIR FRESHENERS AND ODOUR CONTROL

AIR FRESHENER
Use a teaspoon of bicarbonate of soda (baking soda), 15 ml (1 tbsp) of vinegar and 570 ml (1 pint) of water. After it stops foaming, mix well, and use in a spray bottle.

REMOVING PAINT FUMES
Absorb the odour of fresh paint by putting a small dish of white vinegar in the room.

AROMATIC VINEGAR AIR FRESHENER
Add approximately 15g ($^3/_4$ oz) each of sage, rosemary, mint, rue and wormwood to 570 ml (1 pint) of wine or cider vinegar. Allow the herbs to stand in the vinegar for about a week in a warm place. Strain and use as an air freshener or to control unpleasant smells.

TO REMOVE COOKING ODOURS
Boil a teaspoon of white vinegar mixed in 275 ml ($^1/_2$ pint) of water to eliminate unpleasant cooking odours.

REMOVING THE SMELL OF ONIONS
A little white vinegar rubbed on your fingers before and after slicing onions will remove the smell of onions quickly.

SPONGE/CLOTH RESTORER
If a sponge, flannel or dishcloth becomes slimy or smelly, soak overnight in a solution of half vinegar/half water. Rinse in clear water and leave to dry.

HAND CLEANER
Remove cooking smells from hands by rinsing them with vinegar and then wash thoroughly with soap and water.

REMOVING THE SMELL OF VOMIT
To rid the smell after an unfortunate bout of sickness, clean the area thoroughly, then place a bowl of vinegar on the floor and leave overnight. This works very well in a car as well, especially in warm weather. Leave the bowl on the floor of the car overnight, with the doors and windows shut.

REMOVING THE ODOUR OF SOUR MILK
Vinegar will remove the smell of milk from carpets and car upholstery. See above.

RIDDING THE AIR OF STALE SMOKE OR PERFUME
Keep vinegar and water solution handy in a spray bottle for use after smokers have left. Even if they're not smoking, the smell can still be a problem. This is also good for clearing the air of residual scent after visitors, wearing foul aftershave or perfume have left.

REMOVING THE SMELL OF ANIMAL URINE
Blot up the urine with a soft cloth and wash several times with lukewarm water. Apply a mixture of equal parts vinegar and cool water. Blot up again, rinse and let dry.

CLEANING HUMIDIFIERS
Rinse out humidifiers every few days and add two tablespoons of vinegar to prevent mould and bacteria forming. Running this in the bathroom with the door and window closed will eliminate mould. Rinse and run again with clean water. It's important to renew the water each time, rather than just topping up the reservoir.

OTHER HOUSEHOLD USES OF VINEGAR

DISINFECTANT
Kill germs in the bathroom by mixing vinegar and water in a spritzer bottle. Apply liberally.

NYLON TIGHTS
When washing your tights, add vinegar to the water to prolong their lifespan.

WAXING A FLOOR
When waxing a floor after scrubbing with a floor stripper, add 275 ml (½ pint) of vinegar to the rinse water. It neutralizes the chemicals and makes the wax or floor finish adhere better.

PAINTING
Paint adheres better to galvanized metal after it has been brushed with vinegar.

FURTHER HOUSEHOLD USES:
Cleaning lunchboxes
Cleaning breadboxes
Cleaning glasses in the dishwasher
Removing onion odour
Removing refrigerator smells
Rubbish disposal
Deodorizing jars
Cleaning bottles
Cleaning hot plates
Removing stains from fine china
Cleaning oven vents and barbecue grills
Easing seized bolts
Dissolving rust
As fabric glue
Removing stickers
Removing dust on fans
Removing coke stains
Removing soap residue
Restoring hairbrushes
De-staticing plastic
Removing wallpaper

Remedying sagging cane bamboo
Removing excess laundry suds
Cleaning film from small necked bottles
Reduces mineral deposits in pipes, kettles and tanks
Making soap with bicarbonate of soda (baking soda)
Anti-fogging glass cleaner

Cooking
& Recipes

CULINARY USES

The first 'proper' cookery book was printed in 1375. It was written by Guillaume Tirel, personal chef to Charles V of France. M Tirel listed a number of recipes using vinegar, including one which used vinegar to soak bread and a mixture of fresh herbs.

From the 15th century onwards printing presses were beginning to produce recipe books for a hungry public. By 1850 over 300 titles had been published, with most of them giving instructions for vinegar making. Mrs Beeton, in her *Book of Household Management*, included several recipes, some of which have been adapted in the recipe section.

Vinegar can reduce bitterness and balance flavours in a dish. As well as the more obvious addition of vinegar to dressings, sauces and pickles that you may already be aware of, here are some other tips (and cautions) for a range of cooking uses. NB. Vinegar will dissolve reactive metals like aluminium, iron, and copper. When cooking with vinegar, use pots and utensils made of stainless steel, glass, enamel, plastic, or wood.

BREAKING DOWN FIBRES IN MEAT
Adding vinegar to marinades or braising liquids breaks down protein fibres, so will help tenderize meat. Make a marinade in the proportion of one-half cup of wine, white, or cider vinegar to a cup of liquid bouillon.

DIET VINAIGRETTES
To cut calories, make vinaigrettes from milder vinegars like balsamic, champagne, fruit or rice wine vinegar. They're less pungent, and you can use a higher ratio of vinegar to oil.

PEELING HARD-BOILED EGGS
It's easier to peel hard-boiled eggs if you add a teaspoon of vinegar and a tablespoon of salt to the water they cook in.

BOILED EGGS WITH NO CRACKS
Boil better eggs by adding two tablespoons of vinegar before boiling. It keeps them from cracking.

COLOUR ENHANCER
Adding vinegar to a pot of water improves the colour of any vegetables you're cooking. It may, however, also destroy some of the nutrients of green vegetables.

TO MAKE A FLUFFIER MERINGUE
For a really fluffy meringue, add ¼ teaspoon of white vinegar to 3 egg whites.

POACHING EGGS
If you are poaching eggs in an ordinary saucepan, add a teaspoon of white or cider vinegar to the water in which you are poaching the eggs. The whites stay better formed, and you can cook more than one at a time.

KEEPING CHEESE FRESH
To keep cheese fresh and moist, wrap it in a cloth dampened in white vinegar and put it into an air-tight wrapping or container.

FLAVOUR BOOSTER
With just a teaspoon of wine vinegar you can perk up a can of soup, gravy or sauce. It adds flavour and tastes fresher.

TASTIER BOILED HAM
Add a little white, cider or wine vinegar to the water in which you boil ham. It will draw out some of the salty taste and improve the flavour.

WHITER FISH

For a less strong 'fishy' flavour, try soaking fish in vinegar and water before cooking. You'll get a whiter, milder tasting fish. Use two tablespoons of white vinegar per quart of water. Let fish fillets soak in it for 20 minutes before cooking.

BUTTERMILK

Make buttermilk by adding a tablespoon of vinegar to a cup of milk and letting it stand for five minutes to thicken.

EASY WINE VINEGAR

This may do as a standby; make wine vinegar by mixing two tablespoons of vinegar with a teaspoon of dry red wine.

REMOVING FISH SCALES

Scale fish more easily by rubbing with vinegar 5 minutes before scaling.

FIRMER GELATINE

Add a teaspoon of white vinegar to any gelatin recipe in hot summer months to keep moulded salads and desserts firm.

TENDER BOILED BEEF

When you boil beef, add a tablespoon or more of wine, white or cider vinegar to the water to soften fibres and make it tender.

TASTY HEALTH DRINKS

Add a teaspoon or two of cider vinegar to vegetable juice to enhance the flavour.

A tablespoon of cider vinegar and honey in hot water is a tasty health drink.

ALTERNATIVE TO LEMON JUICE

Try using cider vinegar where lemon juice is required e.g. in making mayonnaise.

BREAKFAST TREAT
Just sprinkle on pawpaw for a refreshing breakfast.

'GO-GO JUICE'
Take 2 cups of white grape juice, 2 cups of apple juice and 1 cup of apple cider vinegar. Mix well and refrigerate. Drink a small cup of it each morning, first thing. Each batch should last a week.

MEAT SOUP STOCK
When making soup stock from bones, squirt in a tablespoon of white vinegar, to help extract all the calcium. There will be no vinegar taste, and most of us can certainly use the additional calcium.

USING UP THE LAST OF THE KETCHUP
To use up all those bits of tomato sauce, ketchup or chutney etc that come in bottles, add some vinegar, oil and shake. The liquid will pour out easily; this makes the base for marinades, if you add a little onion, garlic and spices.

DE-GASSING BEANS
De-gas, or lower the amount produced from dried beans by adding a tablespoon of cider vinegar to the soaking water. Leave overnight, then rinse thoroughly. Also add a little to the water when you cook them. This works for split peas as well.

REDUCING BACTERIA
Some people like to wash any flesh foods with vinegar before cooking to reduce the bacteria, especially in chicken, and claim it makes the foods more pleasant to work with.

RINSING FRESH FRUIT AND VEGETABLES
Rinse fresh fruit and vegetables in vinegar. There are, apparently products available for this purpose, but vinegar works as well, and is cheaper.

REMOVING CREEPY CRAWLIES FROM YOUR LETTUCE

A little vinegar and salt added to the water you wash leafy green vegetables in will float out bugs and kill germs.

REDUCING STARCH IN PASTA

If you put a few drops of vinegar in pasta as it boils, the starch is cut. This makes the pasta less sticky.

REDUCING STARCH AND STICKINESS FROM RICE

Use a splash of vinegar when preparing rice, in the proportions of 1 cup of rice, 2 cups of water, a splash of vinegar. Bring to a boil then cover and simmer or let it stand for 20 minutes. Uncover the rice and fluff with a fork. The vinegar cuts the starch and the rice is not sticky.

SUBSTITUTE FOR SOUR MILK OR BUTTERMILK

If you have a recipe that needs sour milk or buttermilk, add a little vinegar to your ordinary milk.

SUBSTITUTE FOR EGGS

When baking, if you find you are short of eggs, substitute one tablespoon of white vinegar per egg. This seems to work for cakes and muffins.

PRESERVING SOUR CREAM

To keep sour cream from spoiling, add one teaspoon of white vinegar to a small container and about two tablespoons to a larger container of sour cream after the first use. You don't notice the taste, and the cream will remain usable for longer.

GENERAL DIRECTIONS FOR MAKING VINEGAR

Winemaking suppliers list acetobacter as mother or vinegar culture. Most suppliers sell red and white wine vinegar cultures. Some sell cider, malt and mead cultures as well. Any culture may be combined with any type alcohol to produce vinegar.

Vinegar should contain at least 5% acid as required for preserving or pickling. Speciality vinegar contains acid as high as 7%. Beer containing 5.5% alcohol will yield about 5% acid. Wine containing 11 to 12% alcohol must be diluted to 5.5 to 7% alcohol before using it to make vinegar.

Acid test kits, sold by winemaking suppliers, are used to determine the acidity of vinegar. Acid tests are easy to perform and instructions come with the kit.

CIDER VINEGAR

If you're feeling adventurous, you might like to try making your own vinegar. There are, however a number of pitfalls regarding any home brewing, ie keeping temperatures constant, preventing wild yeasts affecting the culture and lack of sterilized conditions for production and storage.

Two factors require special attention when making vinegar at home; oxygen supply and temperature. Oxygen is spread throughout the mixture by stirring it daily and by letting air reach the fluid through a muslin (cheesecloth) filter, which is used in place of a lid. The temperature of fermenting cider should be kept between 60 and 80°F (16 and 27°C). Lower temperatures do not always produce usable vinegar, and higher ones interfere with the formation of the 'mother of vinegar' (see The Science of Vinegar Production).

Do not use a metal container when making vinegar; acid in the mixture will corrode metal or aluminium objects. Glass, plastic, wood, enamel or stainless steel containers should be used for making or storing vinegar.

HOW TO MAKE CIDER VINEGAR

MAKING CIDER

Cider needs to be made in autumn, when the apples are full of sugar. The fruit should be checked over and washed well to remove debris. Crush the fruit to produce apple pulp and strain off the juice. You can sometimes get a fruit farm to do this for you, to save a lot of effort. If not, use a press or muslin (cheesecloth) for straining.

If you add yeast to activate the fermentation it will speed up the process. This is not essential, but special cultivated yeasts are available for this purpose at wine-making shops. Don't use bread yeasts. To make a starter, crumble one cake of yeast into a litre (1³/₄ pints) of cider. This makes enough starter for 20 litres (5 gallons) of cider; adjust the proportions of the recipe when making more, or less.

MAKING ALCOHOL AND ACETIC ACID

Pour all of the liquid into containers to about three-quarters capacity, leaving the containers open and stir the mixtures daily. Keep the containers away from direct sunlight and maintain the temperature at 60 to 80°F (16 to 27°C). Full fermentation will take about 3 to 4 weeks. Near the end of this period, you should notice a vinegar-like smell. Taste samples daily until it reaches the desired strength.

FILTERING

When the vinegar is fully fermented, filter the liquid through several layers of fine muslin (cheesecloth) or filter paper; coffee filters work well for this. This process removes the mother of vinegar, and prevents further fermentation of the product, which could spoil it.

STORAGE

Stored vinegar will stay in excellent condition almost indefinitely if it is pasteurized. To do this, heat the vinegar before pouring it into sterilized bottles, then place the bottles in a hot water bath. In both cases, the temperature of the vinegar must reach at least 140°F (60°C) to sterilize the product, and should not exceed 160°F (71°C). Use a cooking thermometer to check the temperature. Cool the containers and store them at room temperature, out of direct sunlight.

STERILIZING

Sterilize utensils and containers that will touch the vinegar by soaking them for 20 minutes in a solution from your supplier, or use baby bottle sterilizers.

VINEGAR METHOD I

3 measures beer, ale or vinegar stock
   (5.5 to 7% alcohol)
1 measure vinegar culture with active bacteria

Use sterilized glass, enamel, stainless steel or stoneware containers less than two-thirds full. Cover the container with a cloth to keep insects out, while allowing air to freely reach the stock. Store the mixture in a dark place.

TEMPERATURES

Temperatures between 80 and 85°F (27–30°C) are ideal. Fluctuating temperatures slow the process, so aim for a fairly constant temperature. At 75 to 85°F (24–30°C) it will take 6 to 8 weeks for conversion. At 85–90°F (30–32°C) it can take 4 to 6 weeks for conversion. Temperatures over 95°F (35°C) slow conversion; above 140°F (60°C) the bacteria die.

An acetic film of mother will form. This smooth, leathery, greyish film becomes quite thick and heavy. Do not disturb! It often becomes heavy enough to fall and may be succeeded by another fermentation. If the mother falls you can then remove and discard it. Use an acid test to indicate when all of the alcohol has been converted to vinegar. You can remove some of the vinegar and pasteurize it (see above). The remaining, unpasteurized vinegar can then be used as a culture to start another batch.

Add beer or diluted wine to the culture every 4 to 8 weeks, depending on the temperature maintained. Adding more alcohol to the culture keeps it alive, prevents spoilage and increases the quality of vinegar. If you expose unpasteurized vinegar to oxygen without alcohol present, the bacteria will convert the vinegar to carbon dioxide and water, and all your hard work will come to nothing.

VINEGAR METHOD II

2 measures dry wine (11 to 12% alcohol)
1 measure water (boiled for 15 minutes and
   allowed to cool)
1 measure vinegar culture with active bacteria

Follow the directions in Method I. You can use
purchased wine, but some commercial wines
contain preservatives that could kill the vinegar
bacteria. Home made wine would be an alternative.

VINEGAR METHOD III

If you are an experienced winemaker, you may like
to follow this method.

Wine containing less than 10% alcohol is subject
to spoilage. This formula to make 7% alcohol
is an ideal vinegar stock. Follow good
winemaking procedures.

When the fermentation is complete (specific gravity
1.000 or below) this low-alcohol wine can be
converted to vinegar as directed in Method I.

680 g (1½ lb) honey (or any sugar source to obtain
   a specific gravity of 1.050)
2 tsp yeast nutrient
4 tsp acid blend (7.5 pt tartaric acid with an acid
   test kit)
¼ tsp tannin
wine yeast
add water to equal 4.5 litres (1 gallon)

USING HOME-MADE WINE

Dry wine containing 11 to 12% alcohol can be diluted after fermentation (specific gravity 1.000 or below). It's important that the wine contains no excess sugar, which will increase the chance of spoilage by a slime-like substance in the vinegar. The wine does not have to be clear as this happens when the vinegar ages. At the last racking, don't add campden tablets or potassium sorbate.

PRESERVING VINEGAR

To preserve vinegar, add 3 campden tablets per 4.5 litres (1 gallon) of vinegar or heat the vinegar to 155°F (68°C) and hold the temperature for 30 minutes. After pasteurizing the vinegar, add one tablespoon of 80% proof vodka to each 4.5 litres (1 gallon) and age it. If you wish to improve the bouquet, add up to one cup of oak or beech chips. Pasteurized vinegar keeps indefinitely when tightly capped and stored in a dark place at room temperature. See below for ageing. Temperatures above 160°F (71°C) cause a loss of acidity, flavour and aroma.

AGEING YOUR VINEGAR

Vinegar has a strong, sharp bite when first made. It becomes mellow when aged for a period of six months or more and when stored at a cool, steady temperature of 50 to 60°F, or 10 to 16°C. This undisturbed rest also allows suspended solids to fall, making the vinegar clear and bright. Siphon the clear vinegar off the deposit of solids into sterilized bottles. Use corks or plastic caps to avoid vinegar contact with metal. If corks are used, make sure that there is an air-tight seal. The quality of vinegar improves for up to two years and then gradually declines.

APPETIZERS AND STARTERS

FRENCH BREAD CANAPÉS

There are several variations to these delicious, crispy accompaniments to an aperitif. The addition of vinegar adds a little tang, and it's a great way to use up stale pieces of bread!

1 large baguette, or similar French stick
150 ml (¼ pint) olive oil
4 garlic cloves, crushed
1 tbsp balsamic vinegar
2 tbsp chopped parsley or other herbs, e.g. basil
225 g (8 oz) grated cheese of your choice
4 or 5 tomatoes

Slice the loaf fairly thickly. Mix garlic with olive oil and brush the bread on both sides with this mixture. Slice the tomatoes thinly and brush with a little oil. Grill the bread on both sides and place a slice of tomato on each piece of toast. Drizzle with balsamic vinegar, sprinkle with chopped herbs, then cheese, and return to the grill until the cheese melts. Serve immediately with a glass of wine.

GOAT CHEESE CANAPÉS

1 long, round goat cheese (if you're really
   adventurous, try the goat cheese recipe overleaf)
½ baguette

Repeat the steps for brushing and toasting the bread, then top each slice of bread with a thin slice of goat cheese. Drizzle over a little balsamic vinegar and return to the grill until the cheese melts and bubbles a little.

RECIPE FOR GOAT CHEESE

Take 13.5 litres (3 gallons) of fresh goat milk and heat for about 45 minutes, stirring constantly. Don't let it boil over. When the milk is hot and foaming, simmer for another 15 minutes. Add 50 ml (3½ tbsp) of vinegar and cook for another 15 minutes, stirring slowly.

Strain through a very clean tea towel. When most of the whey is drained, add a teaspoon of salt and stir into the cheese. Grab all the edges and middle of the towel, wrap a rubber band around the top and then hang from a kitchen cabinet, with a bowl underneath it, as the remaining whey drains out. This should take an hour or so.

The cheese should be cool and hard.

Remove the cloth and place in an air-tight bag and refrigerate.

It is now ready to eat on sandwiches, with pasta, use on pizzas etc.

The vinegar separates the cheese from the whey and the cheese doesn't taste of vinegar.

ASPARAGUS APPETIZER

To serve 4 to 6 people. Trim 1 kg (2.2 lb) asparagus and rinse well to remove any sand. Steam, or cook or them in a large wide saucepan in gently boiling water for 5 to 8 minutes or until tender, but not limp. Alternatively tie bundles of about 8 spears together and stand upright in a tall pot with an inch or so of boiling water, covered, for about 10 minutes.

Rinse under cold water, then serve cold with a vinaigrette (see section on Dressings and Vinaigrettes, overleaf). This is the way we eat them in France. If you prefer a hot dish, serve with a butter sauce.

Light butter sauce
5 ml (1 tsp) finely chopped shallots
15 ml (1 tbsp) white wine vinegar
75 ml (5 tbsp) light sour cream
30 ml (2 tbsp) butter

Cook the shallots in the vinegar in a small saucepan over medium heat until the vinegar has all but evaporated. Reduce the heat to low, then remove altogether from the heat. Stir in the sour cream until blended. Gradually stir in small pieces of butter and serve warm. These can be made in advance and reheated.

(You could miss out the butter, if you need to cut down, and just call it a light sauce!)

AVOCADO AND TOMATO SALAD
2 large, ripe avocado pears
4 large ripe tomatoes
60 ml (4 tbsp) olive oil
15 ml (1 tbsp) balsamic vinegar
Salt and freshly ground pepper
1 tsp English mustard
1 tbsp mixed herbs, chives or basil
Juice of a lemon

Halve and stone the avocados and slice thinly. Sprinkle with the lemon juice to prevent discoloration. Thinly slice the tomatoes and arrange with the pears in a dish. If you have the time, you can make pretty designs with alternating fruits, but I'm usually in a hurry, or the pears don't slice properly. The result is the same anyway, and looks and tastes delicious. Mix the dressing ingredients (not the herbs) in a screw-top jar and shake until they have combined. Pour over the fruit, then sprinkle the herbs on top. This will serve 4–6 people.

AVOCADO, TOMATO AND MOZZARELLA SALAD
1 small mozzarella cheese per person.
Other ingredients as above.

As a more substantial alternative, or as a main course salad dish, add slices of mozzarella cheese with the pears and tomatoes. Very Italian, very yummy.

DRESSINGS AND VINAIGRETTES

We all know that vegetables and salads are good for us, but not everyone likes the taste of raw vegetables, and cooked ones can be bland. As a rule of thumb, you need 3 parts oil to one part vinegar. Different combinations obviously give a range of different flavours which can either complement the food, or completely overpower it. Blander foods such as bean salads need a stronger, sharper mixture. Choose a low-fat or fat-free vinaigrette, and the dressing will make each crunch on those nutrient-rich veggies more enjoyable.

BASIC DRESSING RECIPE
60–90 ml (4–6 tbsp) olive oil, or sunflower oil
15 ml (1 tbsp) cider, wine or balsamic vinegar
15 ml (1 tbsp) lemon juice
1 large garlic clove, crushed
1 large pinch of mustard
Salt and pepper

The easiest way to combine these is to place all the ingredients into a clean, screw-top jar and shake to blend. The dressing can be made in advance, and even stored in the refrigerator for later. On removing from the refrigerator, the dressing may look cloudy. Allow the oil to reach room temperature before shaking again and serving.

FRENCH DRESSING
Use 3 parts olive oil to one part wine vinegar. Add a teaspoon of French mustard, a clove of garlic, a teaspoon of caster (superfine) sugar, salt and pepper. Shake together and serve.

SWEET-AND-SOUR SALAD DRESSING
60g (2½ oz) sugar
30 ml (2 tbsp) rice wine vinegar
1 tbsp diced onion
¼ tsp garlic salt
Salt and pepper
120 ml (8 tbsp) vegetable oil

Combine the sugar, vinegar, onion, salts and pepper and blend until smooth. Pour in the oil in a slow, steady stream and mix until smooth, or use a screw-top jar to shake and mix.

SHERRY VINEGAR AND MUSTARD DRESSING
Sherry vinegar is twice as potent as wine vinegar. Try it with quartered tomatoes, on a white bean salad, or in a mustardy vinaigrette.

Whisk 15 ml (1 tbsp) of sherry vinegar with a teaspoon of Dijon mustard, 75 ml (5 tbsp) of extra virgin olive oil and a pinch of sea salt.

As a refreshing tonic, add a few drops to a glass of iced water

MINT AND HONEY DRESSING
Use 45 ml (3 tbsp) of olive oil, 60 ml (4 tbsp) of cider vinegar, 15 ml (1 tbsp) of clear honey and one of chopped, fresh mint. Add salt and pepper and shake together until blended. This goes well with watercress salad.

MAYONNAISE
Put one egg yolk with salt and pepper in a bowl. Add 150 ml (¼ pint) of olive oil, drop by drop, beating all the time. As it thickens, keep adding the oil, then 5–10 ml (1–2 tsp) of cider vinegar or white wine vinegar. Mix thoroughly.

MAYONNAISE VARIATIONS
Add a large pinch of dry mustard powder with the salt and pepper, or garlic, or tarragon.

For a lower-fat mayonnaise, mix equal quantities of mayonnaise with natural (plain) yogurt.

To avoid eggs, use 1–2 tbsp soya flour, blended with 5 ml (1 tsp) of honey instead of the egg yolk.

SESAME SEED DRESSING
15 ml (1 tbsp) butter
3 tbsp sesame seeds
180 ml (6.3 fl oz) oil; either olive or sunflower
80 ml (2.8 fl oz) white wine vinegar
1 tsp sugar
Salt and pepper

Melt the butter in a small saucepan and sauté the sesame seeds until golden. Let this cool, and then add the other ingredients and mix well.

RASPBERRY AND SESAME DRESSING
75 ml (5 tbsp) raspberry red wine vinegar
10 ml (2 tbsp) clear honey
1 tsp sesame seeds
Salt and pepper
75 ml (5 tbsp) sunflower or olive oil
1 tsp French mustard

Mix all ingredients together in a screw-top jar until well blended. Serve over your favourite salad.

ITALIAN DRESSING WITH SOUR CREAM
This is definitely not for weight watchers!

110 ml (5 fl oz) mayonnaise
110 ml (5 fl oz) sour cream
30 ml (2 tbsp) milk
15 ml (1 tbsp) vinegar
1 garlic clove, crushed
½ tsp dried marjoram
½ tsp dried basil
½ tsp honey
¼ tsp salt
Black pepper

Combine all ingredients into a clean, screw-top jar.
Shake until all the ingredients appear to have
mixed. Leave in the refrigerator for at least 2 hours
before serving, but take out the jar about ten
minutes before you want to use the dressing and
give it another shake.

SALAD DRESSING FOR DIETERS
150 ml (¼ pint) white wine
1 tsp cornflour (cornstarch)
15 ml (1 tbsp) white wine vinegar
1 tbsp chopped parsley
¾ tsp salt
1 tsp poppy seeds

Combine the wine and cornflour in small saucepan
and cook, stirring constantly, until mixture boils
and clears. Remove from the heat and stir in the
remaining ingredients. Cool before using. Serve
with celery hearts, sliced mushrooms or raw
courgette (zucchini).

MARINADES

Flavour enhancers can serve the same purpose for low-fat meats as for vegetables. Spice things up a bit with, garlic, ginger, balsamic vinegar, chilli paste, honey, mustard, spices and herbs. Here are a few suggestions.

MARINADE AND COOKING SAUCE FOR KEBABS

60 ml (4 tbsp) olive oil
15 ml (1 tbsp) balsamic vinegar
1 tsp English mustard
Salt and pepper

This baste and marinade is a family favourite, whether on lamb kebabs or vegetarian versions. The lamb and vegetables remain moist and succulent. I usually use cherry tomatoes, small whole mushrooms, squares of green or red (bell) peppers and baby onions. Leg of lamb, cut into cubes is optional.

APRICOT BARBECUE SAUCE

1 jar (12 oz) apricot preserves
60 ml (4 tbsp) red wine vinegar
1 tsp salt
1 medium garlic clove, crushed
3 tbsp brown sugar
2 tbsp mustard

Blend all ingredients until smooth. Smooth on to chicken or spareribs and leave in a cool place before cooking.

ORIENTAL MARINADE AND BASTE FOR BEEF
60 ml (4 tbsp) white wine
150 ml (¼ pint) chicken broth
70 ml (5 tbsp) soy sauce
⅛ tsp garlic powder
45 ml (3 tbsp) wine vinegar
30 ml (2 tbsp) honey

Shake all ingredients together in a screw-top jar.
Marinate strips of steak for several hours in the
sauce before grilling. Baste meat with the sauce
while cooking.

MARINADE FOR CHICKEN
150 ml (¼ pint) malt vinegar
120 ml (8 tbsp) dry white wine
2 large shallots, thinly sliced
2 tbsp fresh herbs or 2 tsp dried mixed herbs

Salt and freshly ground pepper to taste
Combine the ingredients in a saucepan and
bring to the boil. Cool before marinating meat.
See below for a recipe.

MARINADE FOR SLOW COOKING BRISKET
500 ml (¾ pint) cider or wine vinegar
500 ml (¾ pint) water
2 tsp salt
¼ tsp black pepper
3 tbsp onion powder
3 bay leaves
6 whole cloves
2 tbsp celery salt
¼ tsp thyme leaves
1 tsp mustard seed

MAIN COURSE DISHES

ROAST SALMON WITH BALSAMIC GLAZE
This is a very special way of preparing baked salmon, and will serve 8 to 10 people.

2 kg (4.4 lb) whole salmon
1 tbsp grated lemon rind
2 garlic cloves, crushed
2 tbsp chopped fresh thyme
45 ml (3 tbsp) olive oil
100 ml (6 tbsp) balsamic vinegar
1 tsp granulated (white) sugar
90 ml (6 tbsp) red wine

Chop together the lemon rind, garlic and thyme. Brush oil over the salmon and inside the cavity. Rub the herb mixture all over. (You can prepare this well ahead and keep refrigerated.)

Preheat the oven to 180°C (350°F). Place the salmon in a baking dish lined with foil and roast for 40 minutes or until the juices run clear.

Meanwhile combine balsamic vinegar, wine and sugar in a saucepan. Bring to a boil and reduce the liquid until syrupy.

Before serving, remove the skin and add any juices to the sauce. Skim off excess fat and serve the fish with the sauce.

CHICKEN WITH MALT VINEGAR
4 chicken legs and thighs
150 ml (¼ pint) malt vinegar
120 ml (8 tbsp) dry white wine
2 large shallots, thinly sliced
2 tbsp fresh herbs or 2 tsp dried mixed herbs
Salt and freshly ground pepper to taste

Combine everything but the chicken and simmer
for 2 minutes in a saucepan. Separate the thighs
from the drumsticks if they are attached. Cool the
marinade then pour over the chicken, cover with
plastic and refrigerate for 8 hours or overnight.
To cook, remove the chicken from the marinade and
arrange in a roasting tin covered with foil, or fry or
barbecue, brushing with the marinade.

SPICED BRISKET
1.5kg (3½ lb) brisket
500 ml (¾ pint) cider or wine vinegar
500 ml (¾ pint) water
2 tsp salt
¼ tsp black pepper
3 tbsp onion powder
3 bay leaves
6 whole cloves
2 tbsp celery salt
¼ tsp thyme leaves
1 tsp mustard seed
113g (4 oz) sugar
4 tbsp seedless raisins

Combine vinegar, water, salt, pepper onion powder,
bay leaves, cloves, celery salt, thyme leaves and
mustard seed to make marinade. Place meat in this
mixture, making sure it is covered with liquid. Cover
and let stand in a large pan for at least 2 hours.
Add the sugar. Simmer over a low heat for 3 hours or
until tender. Remove the meat to a plate and keep
hot. Strain the liquid to remove the spices and return
to the saucepan. Stir in the raisins and cook until
thick. Serve with potato dumplings.

WARM CHICKEN SALAD WITH RASPBERRY VINEGAR

2 skinless chicken breast fillets
12 baby spinach leaves
45 ml (3 tbsp) olive oil
45 ml (3 tbsp) pine nuts
15 ml (1 tbsp) raspberry red wine vinegar
15 ml (1 tbsp) white wine vinegar
A handful, about 50 g (2 oz) small lettuce
    leaves, torn
Pepper

Cut the chicken into fine strips. Wash and dry the spinach leaves. Heat 30 ml (2 tbsp) of the olive oil in a small saucepan. Stir-fry the chicken for several minutes, until thoroughly cooked. Add the spinach and cook for about one minute, or until barely wilted. Add the pine nuts and cook for another minute. Spoon the contents of the pan on to serving plates. Pour the vinegars into the pan with the remaining tablespoon of oil, seasoning with pepper, and stir until mixed. Lightly toss with the torn lettuce leaves. Pour over the mixture on the plates and serve immediately.

POTATO SALAD

This is a good salad for barbecues. If you like beetroot (beets), you can add a small cooked one to the potatoes.

4 medium potatoes, unpeeled
30 ml (2 tbsp) raspberry red wine vinegar, or other favourite vinegar
30 ml (2 tbsp) peanut oil or olive oil
15 ml (1 tbsp) lemon juice
1 garlic clove, crushed
Finely chopped fresh parsley
3 spring onions (scallions), chopped
1 tbsp chopped fresh dill
2 tbsp finely chopped fresh mint
Pepper to taste
Paprika

Cook the potatoes for about 20 minutes, until tender. Drain but do not peel, and dice as soon as cool enough to handle. Place in a serving bowl. Put the vinegar, oil, lemon juice and garlic in a screw-top jar and shake until combined. Mix the dressing lightly with the potatoes and allow to cool. When completely cool, toss in the parsley, onions, dill, mint and pepper. Serve at room temperature, sprinkled with a little paprika. (You can vary the herbs as you like.)

STORE SAUCES AND PRESERVING

Some of these recipes are very old, dating from Victorian times or earlier, when they were much in demand, before the impact of refrigeration.

I remember as a child, in the late 1950s, the ranges of pickle jars and surplus garden produce that was either salted or pickled to preserve for the winter months before we had a freezer, although even Mrs Beeton recommended buying pickling vinegar and ready-made pickles, due to their availability and cheap price, way before then.

We used my grandmother's copy of *Mrs Beeton's Book of Household Management*, which I still have today. It's a fascinating historical document, and I can only pity the poor kitchen maids who had to prepare the vegetables and boil vinegar to preserve eggs, oysters, onions, tomatoes, mushrooms, nasturtium seeds, lemons, limes, melons and just about any other fruit or vegetable you can think of.

Mrs Beeton also acknowledged the hit-and-miss nature of using inferior-quality vinegars derived from wood, and the need to use only the best fruit or vegetables for pickling. If nothing else, they should clear the sinuses and make your pans very clean and shiny!

The following recipes can be used as a basic pickling or store sauce for just about any vegetables.

Make sure that you don't let the vinegar make direct contact with metal lids, as erosion can occur.

PARLEY, SAGE, ROSEMARY AND THYME VINEGAR

570 ml (1 pint) red wine vinegar
6 sprigs fresh parsley
1 tsp thyme leaves
1 tsp rosemary leaves
I tsp sage leaves

Thoroughly wash the fresh herbs and dry well. Place vinegar, parsley, thyme, rosemary and sage in a saucepan and bring to a boil. Reduce the heat and simmer for 5 minutes. Cool, then pour mixture into a large clean jar. Cover tightly and set aside for 2 weeks, shaking occasionally. Strain out the herbs through a sieve, then pour the vinegar into bottles with tightly fitting covers. Add a sprig of parsley or rosemary to garnish, if desired. You can use this in salad dressings, marinades or sprinkled over vegetables.

TARRAGON VINEGAR

This popular herb vinegar is used to make sauce and vinaigrettes. Don't add too much tarragon to the bottle, or you may reduce the acidity of the vinegar so much that it loses its ability to preserve. The sprigs will eventually become bitter, so remove or replace them after a few weeks. Make sure that the vinegar you use has an acidity level of at least 5%.

Use 1 tbsp of fresh tarragon leaves plus 225 ml (8 fl oz) of white wine vinegar, champagne vinegar, or apple cider vinegar.

If you use dried tarragon, use one teaspoon of dried leaves plus one cup of vinegar.

CAMP VINEGAR

Add one head of garlic, sliced, 25 g (1 oz) of cayenne pepper, 10 ml (2 tsp) soy sauce and 10 ml (2 tsp) walnut ketchup to 570 ml (1 pint) of vinegar. Allow to infuse in a clean bottle or jar for 4 weeks, then strain the clear liquid into clean, well-sealed bottles.

BASIL AND CINNAMON VINEGAR

50 g (2 oz) basil leaves, plus some with any
   blossoms for garnish
1 cinnamon stick
570 ml (1 pint) white-wine vinegar

Wash the basil and put them in a very clean screw-top jar. Bruise them with a wooden spoon. Add the cinnamon and the vinegar and let the mixture steep, covered, in a cool dark place for 1 to 2 weeks. Strain the vinegar through a fine sieve, pour into clean bottles or jars. Add the basil sprigs saved for garnish and seal the jars.

SAGE AND CARAWAY VINEGAR

50 g (2 oz) fresh sage leaves plus sprigs for garnish
1 tsp caraway seeds
425 ml ($^3/_4$ pint) cider vinegar
150 ml ($^1/_4$ pint) water

Wash the sage leaves, bruise with a rolling pin, or mortar and pestle and place in a very clean screw-top glass jar. Crush the caraway seeds and add to the sage, vinegar and water. Let the mixture steep, covered with the lid, in a cool dark place for 1 to 2 weeks. Strain the vinegar through a fine sieve into clean jars or bottles, discarding the solids. Add the sage sprigs and seal the jars.

JALAPENO GARLIC VINEGAR

2 Jalapeño peppers
2 garlic cloves, crushed
570 ml (1 pint) wine or apple cider vinegar

Cut small slits in the peppers, and place in a clean pint jar with the garlic. Heat the wine or apple cider vinegar to just below the boiling point. Fill a clean jar with vinegar and cap tightly. Allow this to stand for 3 to 4 weeks in a cool dark place. Strain the vinegar, discarding the peppers and garlic, and pour into a sterilized jar. Seal tightly.

Use in dressing for taco, tomato and onion salads, or when making salsa.

CELERY VINEGAR

225 g (8 oz) finely shredded celery, or 25 g (1 oz)
    celery seeds
570 ml (1 pint) pickling vinegar
1 level tsp salt

Boil the vinegar and dissolve the salt in it. Pour the liquid over the celery or celery seed. When cold, cover and leave for 3 weeks. Strain and bottle, sealing securely.

CRESS VINEGAR

Bruise 25 g (1 oz) cress seed and put in vinegar which has been boiled and cooled. Infuse for 2 weeks, then strain and bottle.

CHEROKEE

570 ml (1 pint) malt vinegar
60 ml (4 tbsp) mushroom ketchup
30 ml (2 tbsp) soy sauce
25 g (1 oz) cayenne pepper
2 garlic cloves, finely crushed or chopped

Put the ingredients into a large bottle, cork tightly and leave for 4 weeks. Strain, or siphon, the clear liquid into clean bottles and seal.

CHILLI VINEGAR

This makes my eyes water, just thinking about it!
I think rubber (latex) gloves to protect your fingers
from those chillies might be a good idea, too.

Cut 50 chillies into halves. Boil 570 ml (1 pint) of
pickling vinegar, allow to cool, then pour over the
chillies. Seal and store.

CUCUMBER VINEGAR

I'm hoping for a bumper crop this year, so this
should come in useful:

Boil 570 ml (1pint) of pickling vinegar with a
teaspoon of white peppercorns and a teaspoon of
salt for 20 minutes. While cooling the vinegar, slice
the cucumbers, unpeeled, into wide necked bottles
or jars. Add 2 sliced shallots, a clove of garlic and
the vinegar. Pour over the vinegar and cover tightly.
Keep for 2 weeks, then strain the liquid into clean
bottles and store in a cool, dry place.

ESCAVEEKE SAUCE

There's certainly a hint of 'eek' here.

570 ml (1 pint) white wine vinegar
Finely grated rind of 1 lemon
6 shallots
2 garlic cloves
1 tbsp coriander seeds
1 tsp ground ginger
$\frac{1}{4}$ tsp salt
1 level tsp cayenne pepper

Grind the coriander with the other dry ingredients
in a mortar and pestle. Boil the vinegar and add
to the rest of the ingredients. When cold, bottle
and seal.

SPICED VINEGAR

575 ml (1 pint) vinegar
25 g(1 oz) black peppercorns
25 g (1 oz) fresh root ginger
25 g (1 oz) salt
7 g (½ oz) allspice
25 g (1 oz) finely chopped shallots
2 garlic cloves, crushed
2 bay leaves

Grind the peppercorns and mix together with all ingredients in a wide necked jar. Cover and allow to rest for a week. Place the jar, opened, in a saucepan of boiling water and simmer for 1 hour. When cold, cover tightly and store.

SHALLOT VINEGAR

This is much more straightforward.

Chop 50 g (2 oz) shallots finely and place in a wide necked bottle or jar. Pour over 570 ml (1 pint) of good vinegar, cover securely and leave for 10 days, shaking daily. Strain through muslin or a coffee filter and rebottle for use.

GARLIC OR SHALLOT PICKLE
This takes time and patience; it is not a
last-minute recipe.

570 ml (1 pint) white wine vinegar
110 g (4 oz) shallots or garlic
25 g (1 oz) fresh root ginger
25 g (1 oz) chillies
50 g (approx 2 oz) mustard seed
25 g(1 oz) turmeric
275 ml (½ pint) water
75 g (3 oz) salt

Firstly, boil the water and salt to create a brine,
then pour over the root ginger. After 5 days,
remove the ginger, slice and dry it and discard the
brine. Meanwhile, peel the shallots or garlic,
sprinkle with salt and leave for 3 days.

Place the ginger, shallots or garlic, chillies, mustard
and turmeric in a wide necked bottle, pour over the
vinegar and cover tightly. Store in a cool, dry place.

PICKLED ONIONS
Easy peasy, and very tasty.

Remove the skins from pickling onions, until the
onions are clear and firm. Place into clean, dry jars
and cover immediately with vinegar. For each 570 g,
or pint, of vinegar used, add a teaspoon of black
peppercorns and a teaspoon of allspice. Cover and
store for 2 weeks, when they will be ready to eat.

PICCALILLI I

Use the Spiced Vinegar recipe on page 102.

Use cauliflower, onions, gherkins, French (green) beans, green (bell) peppers, mustard, turmeric and curry powder. Cut the vegetables into small chunks and cook in boiling, strongly salted water for 3 minutes. Drain cool and allow the vegetables to dry thoroughly on large plates. Add a large pinch of turmeric and curry powder to each pint of the spiced vinegar recipe. Take 15 g ($\frac{1}{2}$ oz) of mustard powder and mix with a little cold vinegar to make a paste. Add this to the spiced vinegar as it cools after the boiling period. Combine all of the ingredients in jars and cover with vinegar. When cold, cover and store.

PICCALILLI II

225 g (8 oz) cauliflower florets
125 g (4$\frac{1}{2}$ oz) French (green) beans
225 g (8 oz) pickling onions
225 g (8 oz) diced cucumber
125 g (4$\frac{1}{2}$ oz) salt
1 tsp turmeric
3 tsp dry mustard
1 tsp ground ginger
75 g (3 oz) sugar
425 ml ($\frac{3}{4}$ pint) malt vinegar
4 tsp cornflour (cornstarch)

Put the vegetables, chopped and sliced, in a colander and add the salt. Leave to stand for as long as possible, then rinse and drain. Mix the ginger, sugar, turmeric and mustard with a little of the vinegar. Add all but a few tablespoons of the remaining vinegar and put in a saucepan with the vegetables. Simmer gently for about 5 minutes. Don't let the vegetables go soggy. Mix the remaining vinegar with the cornflour, add to the pan with the vegetables and bring to the boil, stirring carefully. After 3 minutes, spoon the mixture into wide necked jars, cool and cover.

RASPBERRY VINEGAR I

Cover raspberries with white wine vinegar and let them remain undisturbed for 4 days. Strain through a sieve carefully, while pressing the fruit. Pour the vinegar over a fresh lot of raspberries and continue as before. Repeat two or three times more.

For every 570 ml (1 pint) of raspberry vinegar, add 350 to 450 g (12 to 16 oz) of sugar. Simmer gently for 10 minutes, skimming off any froth. Cool and bottle.

RASPBERRY VINEGAR II

Put equal measures of raspberries and vinegar into a large jar and stir the mixture two or three times a day for 10 days. Strain off the vinegar, add 350 g (12 oz) sugar to each 570 ml (1 pint) and bring to the boil. Skim well and when cold, bottle for use in salad or fruit recipes, or dilute with mineral water for a refreshing drink.

STRAWBERRY VINEGARS

2 punnets fresh strawberries
40 fl oz (2 pints) cider vinegar
125 g (4½ oz) sugar

Remove stems from strawberries; halve strawberries; set 4 tablespoons aside. Place remaining strawberries into a large bowl. Pour vinegar over strawberries. Cover and set aside for 1 hour. Transfer vinegar and strawberries to a large sauce pot. Add sugar and bring to a boil. Reduce heat and simmer, covered, for 10 minutes. Strain out strawberry mixture, pressing out as much liquid as possible. Pour vinegar into a 2 pint jar. Add reserved strawberries. Cover tightly. A tablespoonful in a glass filled with 225 g (8 oz) of club soda and ice makes a delightfully cooling drink. Also a creatively different basting sauce for chicken, duck or pork.

DESSERTS AND FRUITY APPETIZERS

STRAWBERRIES BALSAMICO
Place small whole, or quartered large, washed strawberries in a bowl. Season with 30—45 ml (2—3 tbsp) of balsamic vinegar. Allow to stand for 15 minutes. Add sugar to taste. Mix well and serve. This is an acquired taste. My dinner guests were a bit surprised by it; maybe I was a bit mean with the sugar!

MELON SORBET
2 ripe sweet melons, halved and de-seeded
90 ml (6 tbsp) white wine vinegar
2 large egg whites
110 g (4 oz) icing (confectioners') sugar, sifted

You need to make this well in advance, preferably the night before you want to eat it. Scoop the flesh from the melons and place in a food processor with the sugar and vinegar. Blend to a purée and place in a freezer-proof container. Cover and freeze for 4—5 hours.

Whisk the egg whites until stiff, then blend with the semi-frozen sorbet. Freeze until solid. Before you serve it, leave to stand at room temperature for 10—15 minutes. Refreshing at the start or end of a meal, or between courses.

SCRAMBLED EGGS
Add a few drops of vinegar into your egg mixture to boost the taste of your scrambled eggs.

FIRMER JELLY
Adding vinegar to your jelly makes it set firmer.

FLUFFIER RICE
Fork through the rice with a few drops of vinegar.

SHINY CRUSTS
Paint over the edges of your pie or bread for shiny crusts.

CAULIFLOWER
Adding a few drops of vinegar to your cauliflower will make it white and clean.

FURTHER COOKING USES AND RECIPES:
Cooking ham
Preservng uncooked ham
Preserving pepper
Preventing discoloration of peeled potatoes
Preventing lump icing
Tender fish
Taking the edge off your appetite
Low calorie ice creams, crisps, snacks, sweets
Thickeners (ice cream and salad dressing)
Weight reduction
Base for artificial meat
Sausage and meat casing
Serum cholesterol reduction
Kombucha elixir
Manchurian tea
Bon bon chicken salad
Asian black bean and asparagus salad
Autumn broccoli salad
Skewered chicken breast
Texas blue cheese slaw
Hummus in pitta pockets
Vinegar cookies
Vinegar pies
Tangy lemon custard tart
Pickled relish platter
Herbed olives and onion marinade
Vinegar cheese
Chicken adobo
Salmon with onion marmalade
Country French caviar

Uses for Health & Personal Care

CIDER VINEGAR AND HEALTH BENEFITS

If an apple a day keeps the doctor away, then using apple cider vinegar should do the trick as well. Apples are among the most health-giving fruits available as they contain a host of nutritious properties, including: phosphorous, potassium, sodium, magnesium, calcium, sulphur, iron, fluorine, silicon, plus many trace elements.

It contributes to healthy veins, blood vessels and arteries. Apple cider vinegar has extraordinary potassium content and beneficial malic acid. When purchasing cider vinegar for health, it should have a fuzzy sediment (mother), on the bottom, proving that the vinegar is still in the live fermentation stage.

CIDER VINEGAR AND BLOOD
Cider vinegar helps with cleansing, the reintroduction of minerals, as well as the clotting of the blood. Oxidation of the blood is very important and cider vinegar is an effective treatment for this.

Amongst other claims, cider vinegar is said to be very effective in detoxifying various organs in the body together with the blood stream. It is a purifier, as it has a means of breaking down fatty, mucous and phlegm deposits within the body, promoting the health of the vital organs of the body e.g. kidneys, bladder, liver etc., by preventing an excessively alkaline urine.

Cider vinegar appears to help oxidize the blood, which consequently prevents the blood from becoming too thick, giving rise to a strained heart and blood vessels because of high blood pressure. Cider vinegar also promotes digestion, and it neutralizes toxic substances.

POTASSIUM

Apple cider vinegar has a potent supply of potassium, which has become so widely acclaimed in helping various complaints, including excessive mucous formation, watery eyes, sinus and catarrhal troubles. Other signs of potassium deficiency may be tooth decay and the splitting of finger nails. Potassium is essential for the normal growth of the body and for replacing worn-out tissues which depend upon the presence of this mineral. It is as important to the soft tissues, as calcium is to the bones and teeth and it also retards the hardening of the blood vessels.

The following suggestions are passed on as possible solutions to a range of minor ailments, or as preventative suggestions for more serious conditions. Obviously, you should seek medical advice if in doubt, or you are taking prescribed medicines already.

ABRASIONS
Vinegar is a natural antiseptic, so use diluted to clean minor cuts or abrasions, and to reduce itch from poison ivy or mosquito bites.

AFTERSHAVE
Relief for skin sensitive to shaving may be at hand. Elderly men who use this method regularly are said to have soft, smooth faces, just like a baby's. This is also good for rashes or pimples. Drink apple cider vinegar, honey and hot water every morning. The vinegar smell goes away very quickly when used as an aftershave.

AFTERSUN TREATMENT
At bedtime, cover sunburns with a towel or tea towel soaked in water and vinegar and try to persuade the patient to sleep this way. Younger ones, of course, will have a struggle with this, especially because of the smell! Repeat with resoaked towels for best results.

Put vinegar in a spray bottle with water and spray on to sunburn. It soothes for quite a length of time.

To relieve swelling and fluid from too much sun, mix a paste of bicarbonate of soda (baking soda) and apple cider vinegar, and apply.

AGE SPOTS
As a remedy for age spots, mix equal parts of onion juice and vinegar and use daily on age spots. This will take a few weeks to work, just like its expensive relative from the store, although you may smell a bit like a crisp (potato chip) bag!

ALLERGY TO DUST MITES

Add 4 fl oz (8 tbsp) vinegar to a gallon of water to keep your vinyl floors clean and shining. Not only does it keep the floors shiny but it kills the dust mites!

ARTHRITIS

Drink a glass of water with two teaspoons of cider vinegar and two teaspoons of honey three times a day. It dissolves the crystal deposits of uric acid that form between joints (and also in muscles as with muscular rheumatism).

Local treatment can also be given by soaking the arthritic hand, or foot in a strong, comfortably hot solution of cider vinegar for ten minutes, two or three times a day. Use a quarter of a cup of cider vinegar to one and a half cups of water. Arthritic knees can be attended to by making a poultice; soak the cloth in a mixture of cider vinegar and water, (as per above mixture) wring out and wrap it around the joint, then secure with a dry cloth to retain heat. When the wet cloth cools, it should be wrung out in the hot solution and applied afresh. Repeat several times, twice daily.

While this seems to be effective, always ask your doctor before attempting to diagnose yourself or deciding upon medication to alleviate any symptoms.

ASTHMA

One tablespoonful of cider vinegar added to a glass of water should be taken in sips for half an hour. After a further half an hour has elapsed the treatment should be repeated. The wheezing should lessen in intensity quite considerably. Deep breathing exercises are also a beneficial treatment. Always seek medical advice if in doubt. This is not intended as a replacement for professional help.

ATHLETE'S FOOT
Try soaking your feet in vinegar and water. It changes skin pH so that the fungus cannot grow. Soak for three evenings in a row.

BOILS
Boils are quite painful and at times have to be lanced. Vinegar tea can help. One tablespoon of cider vinegar and one tablespoon of honey mixed in a cup of hot water at least twice a day as well as plenty of water may bring relief. Stay away from sodas and chocolate, as they seem to aggravate the infected area even more. If the boil does come to a head where it is going to open, continue to drink the vinegar tea and the water. Use hot packs on the boil for 15–20 minutes three times a day. Doing this has more than once saved an unwanted visit to the doctor. What is also important is not to squeeze a boil.

BONES
The manganese, magnesium, silicon and calcium found in apple cider vinegar have been linked in sustaining bone mass, which is important in the fight against osteoporosis. A supplement of apple cider vinegar could, for this reason, be valuable should you suffer from a calcium shortage, or if you are entering your postmenopausal stage, where a risk of bone density loss could cause a problem.

BRUISES, STIFFNESS AND SWELLING
For a stiff neck, take a half vinegar half warm water solution and soak a rag in it, then wring the rag out and wrap it around your neck. Put a layer of plastic wrap (to keep your sheets dry) and finish up with a towel. Be careful not to strangle yourself! Leave this on overnight and in the morning you will not believe the difference.

For bruises and swelling follow the directions above, but use cold water. You can hold the compress in place with a bandage. Leave on for at least an hour, but the longer you leave it the better the results. This can be effective long after ice ceases to reduce the swelling.

CALCIUM SUPPLEMENT, CLEOPATRA-STYLE
Soak rinsed, dried and crushed egg shells in vinegar until they dissolve. You need about 12 shells to every litre of organic apple cider vinegar. Use a strong jar, with room for expansion of gases. This may take some time. Dilute with water, and drink your calcium supplement.

Oyster shells can also be dissolved in vinegar until dissolved, then drunk, for a calcium supplement.

CLEANSING LOTION
Use vinegar diluted 50/50 as a skin cleanser. Most soaps are alkaline compared to skin pH, so this redresses the balance.

Or, pour 30 ml (2 tbsp) of vinegar into your rinse water, rinse the face and let it air dry. This seals the moisture in the skin and is great for all-over, especially when the weather is dry.

CORNS AND CALLUSES
This old remedy for corn and callus removal involves soaking a piece of stale bread (a cloth would probably do as well) in vinegar, and taping it over the callus or corn overnight.

COLDS

The pH factor (the acidity factor) of the body becomes a bit more alkaline prior to a cold or flu striking you down. When you take cider vinegar it helps to rebalance the acid level of your body.

Another remedy for colds and flu, and said to be specifically beneficial for chest complaints during the winter, is to soak a piece of brown paper with apple cider vinegar, and to place pepper on the one side of the paper. You then tie the paper, pepper side down, on to your chest and leave on for 25–30 minutes. Are there any volunteers?

COLD SORES

If you douse your cold sore repeatedly with vinegar, it will dry up the cold sore and eventually prevent further outbreaks.

CONSTIPATION

As we age our bodies produce less digestive acids (hydrochloric acid), pepsin and digestive enzymes – which can cause constipation. When you add fibre to your diet, such as the pectin in cider vinegar, you assist your body by having regular bowel movements.

CRAMPS

If you have never woken up in the middle of the night with cramps tearing through your calves, feet or legs, you would not understand the agony. A useful remedy to assist with this is to take cider vinegar before going to bed.

To relieve muscle cramps, use half vinegar and half water on a wet towel. Heat in a microwave for 20 seconds and place on the affected area.

COLITIS

The cider vinegar and honey treatment has been used effectively in the treatment for colitis. Take the normal dosage of 10 ml (2 tsp) of cider vinegar and honey with water, three times a day.

COUGHS

There are many types of coughs, and these should be treated with reference to their nature and intensity. However, the vinegar and honey treatment may help some types.

TICKLY COUGH

Two teaspoons of cider vinegar and two of honey mixed with a glassful of water should be taken before meals, or when the irritation occurs. In the evening it would be an idea to have this mixture by your bed so that it can be sipped during the night.

For a cough that will not stop, make a remedy called Witches Brew. Mix one tablespoon of butter, one of sugar and one of vinegar. Melt it all together, and take while still warm.

If you are really brave, or desperate, try this one. Relieve a cough by mixing half a cup of apple cider vinegar, half a cup of water, one teaspoon of cayenne pepper, and four teaspoons of honey. Take a tablespoon when the cough starts and another tablespoon at bedtime.

DIABETES

This disease is becoming more and more common and needs proper medical supervision. It is, however, interesting to note that added dietary fibre, such as contained in cider vinegar, is beneficial in controlling blood glucose levels.

DIARRHOEA

Cider vinegar helps with the digestion, and is an antiseptic to the intestines and the whole of the digestive tract. Due to its healing properties, diarrhoea can be controlled in a very short time, unless some serious physical disorder is apparent.

One teaspoonful of cider vinegar in a glass of water should be taken before and in between meals i.e. approximately six glasses during the course of the day. Please note, however, that diarrhoea is a natural attempt on the part of the body to eliminate some poison which is irritating the digestive tract. Cider vinegar will lessen the intensity, and allow the natural course of elimination to take place.
A testimonial for vinegar I read recently reported another grandma who used to give a straight teaspoon of vinegar to stop diarrhoea. Normally once the vinegar was taken the visits to the toilet stopped after about 30 minutes — or perhaps the vinegar was worse than the frequent visits to the loo!

DEODORANT

Try white vinegar underarms and other areas of the body as a natural deodorant. It won't stop perspiration (which is not healthy anyway) but it will neutralize any odour.

DEPRESSION

Some Eastern medicines believe that depression is the symptom of a stagnant or tired liver. If you believe in this philosophy, then apple cider vinegar would help to fight depression, since it is a great medium to help detoxify and clean the liver.

DIZZINESS

Two teaspoons of apple cider vinegar together with two teaspoons of honey in a glass of hot or cold water three times a day may help this annoying occurrence quite considerably.

EAR DISCHARGE

The treatment for this complaint, which usually occurs during childhood is one teaspoonful of cider vinegar in a glass of water to be drunk mid-morning and mid-afternoon. The discharge should shortly disappear.

An old remedy which may help where all else has failed is to use an ear wash. Use any vinegar, white is fine, and mix in equal amounts with water. Warm slightly so you don't screw up your equilibrium by putting cold water in your ear. Be sure not to make it too warm. Flush the affected ear 2–3 times with the mixture twice a day. Don't be tempted to stick cotton wool or buds in!

ECZEMA

Take the usual dosage of cider vinegar and honey in a glassful of water three times a day, with meals. An application of well diluted cider vinegar can also be applied to the skin several times daily, i.e. one teaspoonful to half a cup of water. Under no circumstances should salt be taken, as this can aggravate the eczema condition considerably.

TIRED AND SORE EYES

The cider vinegar therapy together with honey is the essential ingredients here. Take two teaspoons of each taken in a glassful of water, three times a day. This mixture retards the onset of tired and sore eyes which are usually apparent in later life, as it supplies them with those vital elements essential to their health and functioning.

FATIGUE

Chronic fatigue is a warning that the body needs some attention. To remedy a poor quality sleep, honey is highly recommended, as it acts as a sedative to the body. Twenty minutes after the honey has been taken into the mouth it has been digested and absorbed into the body. This is because it is a predigested sugar, already digested in the stomach of the honey bee, and it requires no effort on the part of the human stomach for digestion. Keep the following mixture by your bedside to be taken as indicated: 15 ml (3 tsp) of apple cider vinegar to 275 ml (½ pint) of honey.

Take 10 ml (2 tsp) of the mixture before retiring. This should induce sound sleep within an hour. If however, you have been unable to sleep within this period, repeat the dosage.

FIGHTING FREE RADICALS

Although cider cannot cure cancer, it is a valuable ally to have around to help fight free radicals in the body, which have been shown to be indicative in the formation of various cancers. Beta-carotene, found in apple cider vinegar, is a powerful antioxidant, which helps in neutralizing the free radicals formed in our bodies.

FOOD POISONING

There have been many cases where people who were in the habit of taking cider vinegar regularly never suffer any side effects from food poisoning. The cider vinegar has an antiseptic quality which seems to render noxious food harmless.

GALLSTONES AND KIDNEY STONES

A theory exist that the acids found in cider vinegar are beneficial in breaking up kidney stones and gallstones, by softening or dissolving them.

HAEMORRHOIDS

Strange as it sounds, vinegar soothes the itching and burning. Just take a cotton ball and dab the affected area with full strength cider vinegar.

Caution: some people find the full strength solution stings. If this happens to you, just dilute the vinegar half and half with water.

HAIR CARE

Although we lose hair daily which is replaced, greater hair loss is primarily due to a tissue salt deficiency, so cider vinegar with its 'wonder products' will re-establish a natural balance, and supply the deficiencies where needed. By taking cider vinegar treatment the hair will maintain its natural growth. This will take approximately two months, so persevere. The dosage is one teaspoonful of cider vinegar to a glass of water to be taken with or between meals. Cider vinegar can also be used externally for the treatment of dandruff (see page 131).

HAIR RINSE

Used as a hair rinse, vinegar neutralizes the alkali left by shampoos. It will give your hair an all out shine, and remove surplus soap. Add a tablespoon or two of vinegar to the final rinse. The smell doesn't linger.

When you have dyed your hair, rinse with warm water then dilute white vinegar with water for the final rinse. Use the water as cold as you can stand. This seals your colour so it doesn't fade out as quickly.

HAY FEVER

This ailment is marked by watery eyes, sneezing and running nose, in other words there is an excess of fluid which the body is drastically trying to offload. For an effective relief, use honey and cider vinegar. Take a tablespoonful of honey after each meal for approximately a fortnight before the onset of the hay-fever season. The ordinary dosage of cider vinegar and honey should then be taken: two teaspoons of cider vinegar and two of honey in a glass of water, three times a day. This dosage should be maintained during the entire hay-fever season.

HEADACHES

There are several types of headache, caused by various reasons. One granny from Scotland apparently used vinegar extensively on a cloth placed on her forehead to stop hangover headaches after weekly get-togethers. Go Granny!

Many people have had relief from headaches by the use of honey. Two teaspoons taken at each meal may well prevent an attack. Another effective means is to mix cider vinegar in equal parts with water. Place in a small basin on the stove, allowing it to boil slowly. When the fumes begin to rise from the basin make a tent with a towel and lean your head over it until the fumes are comfortably strong. Inhale deeply and slowly. (If it makes you cough, cut back on the vinegar.) Generally this alleviates the headache considerably, if not entirely.

HEADLICE

It is also helpful when children get lice, if you take warm vinegar and put it on the hair. Also take your nit comb and dip it in the vinegar. As you run it through the hair it helps remove the nits. It is supposed to be able to help break down the glue the nits use to stay attached to the hair. Use the treatment on the whole family.

HEART
Since cider vinegar is used to promote the health of veins and capillaries, the potassium content in apple cider vinegar is also useful in assisting in the health of the heart and blood pressure.

HEARTBURN
This usually occurs after eating, sometimes up to two hours later. This very unpleasant feeling can be alleviated by taking the usual dosage of cider vinegar and water before meals.

HEALING WOUNDS
Cider vinegar can help the blood to clot more easily. For extra efficiency a very weak solution of cider vinegar with water can be applied to the sore, wound or cut. Poultices of cider vinegar (see instructions under the heading Arthritis, page 113) can be applied to a stubborn open wound.

HICCOUGHS
These have been known to be eradicated by drinking a teaspoon of cider vinegar neat!

Gargling with cider vinegar will reportedly stop the most horrible case of hiccoughs.

Alternatively cider vinegar with water can be taken before mealtimes to prevent this occurrence. Rinse out the mouth after drinking vinegar.

HIGH BLOOD PRESSURE
Emphasis for sufferers is on the natural, foods which are given in the form of fresh fruits, vegetables and honey — rather than the high protein foods which include eggs, meat, milk, cheese, nuts, beans etc. A balance must be maintained between proteins and carbohydrates. The following dosage should be taken daily: two teaspoons of apple cider vinegar and honey in a glass of water — up to three to four times a day.

HOT FLUSHES

Taking one or two teaspoons of vinegar with a glass of water three times a day or more may ease the symptoms, until the hot flushes are gone.

INDIGESTION

When people start talking about indigestion they immediately start referring to the excess stomach acid that they have, although in most cases it is a case of a shortage of it.

Hydrochloric acid and pepsin, an enzyme working in an acid environment, are needed to break down the food effectively. Taking apple cider vinegar may assist in effecting a remedy. Put a capful of vinegar in a glass of water. It gets rid of gassy, bloating or diarrhoea problems. It seems to help balance the acid needed for digestion.

INFECTED PIERCINGS

I can't speak from experience, but was interested in an anecdote from a 'victim'. Warm vinegar applied to a belly button, ear or nose piercing can act as a natural antiseptic if you run out of the antiseptic supplied. Soak the affected area regularly for about three days. Always seek medical advice if in doubt.

INSECT REPELLENT

Drink a couple of spoonfuls a day to keep mosquitoes away — your perspiration will be unpleasant to mosquitoes.

If you rub or spray yourself with vinegar, it will keep ticks off. They may get on you, but will not stay ... and no, once it dries, you do not smell like a vinegar bottle.

INSOMNIA

There have been excellent results with the cider vinegar and honey treatment as follows: two teaspoons of cider vinegar and two of honey in a glass of water to be taken before retiring. It would also be beneficial to have a glass of this mixture by the bedside to sip if needed.

IRRITABLE BOWEL

This is certainly worth thinking about when dealing with symptoms of irritable bowel syndrome.
Sip water with apple cider vinegar during the day. It works for some people, and would certainly be worth trying for those who experience this distressing problem.

KIDNEYS AND BLADDER

The kidneys and bladder can benefit tremendously by a 'flushing', received when the following cider vinegar therapy is undertaken: two teaspoons of cider vinegar in a glass of water six times a day. It would be beneficial to drink a couple of glasses of water in the morning, taking one teaspoonful of cider vinegar in each drink. Comfrey tea, first thing in the morning with a teaspoon of cider vinegar also creates a cleansing action.

MENOPAUSE

If taking calcium-magnesium tablets/or powder, wash it down with something acidic like vinegar diluted in water, so that it will dissolve the calcium magnesium and your body can assimilate it quickly.

METABOLISM

Cider vinegar has been used for centuries in aiding the liver to detoxify the body and to help with digesting rich, fatty and greasy foods, and for proper metabolizing of proteins, fats and minerals.

An added extra to help with this is the malic acid and tartaric acid found in cider vinegar, since they help to bring the acid content into balance, while killing off unfriendly bacteria in the digestive tract.

MINOR BURNS

When cooking, splash some white vinegar on a bit of paper towel and put it on the burn. It stops hurting immediately and if you keep it on, you will not develop a blister.

MUSCLES

By adding some cider vinegar to your diet, you could assist the body to get rid of lactic acid at a faster pace, since it will help to break down the acid crystals, making it much easier to be flushed out of the body.

Use 2 cups of cider vinegar in the bath to soak sore muscles and add potassium to muscles.

NASAL CONGESTION

Many sufferers of nasal congestion have experienced relief by adding apple cider vinegar to their diet.

NAUSEA

Sip on one teaspoon in ½ to 1 cup of water. Honey may be added if desired to enhance the flavour.

NOSE BLEEDS

If a person has a nose bleed without any apparent reason, then two teaspoons of cider vinegar in a glass of water, three times a day will aid in restoring the natural clotting properties of the blood.

PEDICURE PAMPERING
Put ½ cup into a bowl to soak your feet in before a pedicure. It softens your skin beautifully.

REDUCING CHOLESTEROL
A good warning system for heart disease is the presence of high blood cholesterol in the system. To help prevent this is to follow a lifestyle which includes eating a diet high in fruits and vegetables, maintaining your ideal weight, getting enough exercise while avoiding processed foods, junk foods and hydrogenated oils.

Another way is to add fibre to your diet, especially water-soluble fibre such as the pectin found in cider vinegar. Water-soluble fibre adds bulk, and also keeps on working longer than non water-soluble fibre. Fibre also soaks up fats and cholesterol in the body and then is excreted instead of being reabsorbed. Many elderly people with high cholesterol have tried this drink with much success.

2 cups of grape juice
1 cup of apple juice
¼ cup of white vinegar

Mix together, chill and drink ½ to one cup before your largest meal everyday.

SKIN RASHES
Cider vinegar can help some itchy skin rashes clear up and relieve itching. Apply 2–3 times a day for two weeks.

Some psoriasis sufferers have found relief after showering by filling a spray bottle with 3 parts cider vinegar and 1 part water. Spray and rinse all over. There is no soap residue left on the skin.

Vinegar baths can be effective, even in young babies when they react to something their mum has eaten. Pour about a cup of apple cider vinegar into the bath water, and watch the results.

SORE THROAT

A gargle made from apple cider vinegar and water could prove to be a great relief for a sore throat — be that a bacterial or virus infection. Use a 50/50 mixture, and spit out the solution after gargling, which should be repeated every hour. After gargling rinse the mouth with clean water to prevent the acid from eroding the enamel on your teeth.

SPRAINS

An old remedy was to mix vinegar with red clay, heat it and make a paste. It was placed on the sprain and then wrapped with strips of an old sheet. After an hour the paste was soaked off with warm water.

Alternatively, try the Jack and Jill remedy for sore heads; soak a brown paper bag in vinegar and wrap it around your foot all night. The swelling should have gone down two thirds, and you may be able to walk on it again within three days.

STIFF JOINTS

A shortage of potassium in the body may cause stiff joints. Apple cider vinegar could help in relieving this problem when ingesting it, since it is a good source of the needed nutrient. Another remedy is to relax in a warm tub, with some apple cider vinegar added to the water.

STINGS

Use vinegar on wasp stings. Just soak a cotton ball in cider vinegar and hold to the sore spot. Within a few minutes the pain stops. It would work on bee stings too, only you'd probably need to get the sting out.

A scuba diver recommends vinegar for treatment to remove the sting of a jellyfish.

TANNING AID

Mix vinegar with baby oil for a tan. It won't, of course protect your skin from harmful rays, but it will make you fry evenly.

TENDONITIS
Soak the effected area in warm cider vinegar twice a day.

TOE NAIL FUNGUS
Medicine for toe nail fungus can be very costly, but you can use one part vinegar to one part warm water and soak your feet.

Put a few drops of white vinegar on the nail several times a day for results.

TOOTHACHE
Soak a cotton ball or piece of paper towel in vinegar and place it on the aching tooth. Bite down; in moments the toothache is temporarily gone, giving you time to get to a dentist. Always rinse your mouth thoroughly after using vinegar, as it deteriorates the enamel.

ULCERS
Cider vinegar is showing great promise in helping to heal alcohol-induced ulcers, since it activates the body to start its own defensive mechanism.

VARICOSE VEINS
Splash vinegar on your varicose veins. The vinegar is supposed to reduce the veins and relieve the pain and swelling. Of course, you might smell like a tossed salad, but not for long.

WART REMOVER
Remove warts by applying a lotion of half cider vinegar and half glycerine. Apply daily to the warts until they dissolve.

WEIGHT LOSS
Cider vinegar has been used as a weight loss remedy for centuries, and although the mechanics are not always clear on how it works, it really does work.

It has been suggested that the apple cider vinegar works because it makes the body burn calories better, that it reduces the appetite, or simply that it gets the entire metabolism working at top efficiency.

But whatever the reason, the fact remains that it has stood the test of time as a fat-busting supplement, and has helped countless people to achieve their ideal weight. Taking a little bit of vinegar with or just before meals isolates the fat in food and it passes through your system.

Combine one tablespoon of apple cider vinegar and one tablespoon of honey in an 8 oz glass of unsweetened grapefruit juice. Drink one glass before each meal as an appetite suppressant.

WHITENING TEETH

Once a week, dip a wet toothbrush in white vinegar and brush your teeth. It does away with any bad breath, especially after eating onions and it also whitens the teeth.

NOTE: Any time you take vinegar internally, be sure to rinse your mouth with plain water. Acid remaining on teeth will eventually, over time, dissolve your teeth, as it does with calcium deposits around the sink.

YEAST INFECTION

Although there are different factors influencing the formation of Candida (which is a yeast infection) a disturbance of your diet, as well as an intake of antibiotics may be responsible. An alternative treatment can be found by bathing twice a day with a solution of ACV until the symptoms disappear. The solution is made from two tablespoons of ACV to a quart of lukewarm water — this solution will assist in restoring the acid balance.

REMOVE DANDRUFF
Wash hair with a mixture of vinegar and water to remove dandruff and add shine to hair.

REMEDY FOR CHAPPED SKIN
Apply to sore spots liberally. Vinegar provides quick healing powers.

SWOLLEN SKIN
Apply as above.

REMOVE FRUIT STAINS
Remove fruit stains from your hands by applying vinegar to them.

DETECTING CERVICAL CANCER
Medical research has indicated that cervical cancer can be detected early on by the use of vinegar.

RELIEVES FOOT ODOUR
Bathe feet in a mixture of water and vinegar to remove odour. The same method can be applied to those with facial acne.

BRITTLE NAILS
Simply apply vinegar directly to treat and strengthen brittle nails.

REMOVES MOSQUITO ITCH
Soak a sponge in vinegar and apply to the bite.

FURTHER HEALTH RELATED USES:
Wound care dressings
Artificial skin substrate
Cosmetics and beauty
Skin creams
Astringents
Base for artificial nails
Thickener and strengthener for fingernail polish

Pets & Animals

REMOVING AND PREVENTING FLEAS

Adding cider vinegar to drinking water discourages fleas from setting up home on dogs and cats. Start with a few drops so that your pet gets used to the taste, then build up a little, to a teaspoon per bowl for a small animal, to a tablespoon for a larger pet.

Alternatively, dip your pet in a bath of cider vinegar and water. This is, apparently, suitable treatment for puppies that are too young for commercial chemical treatments. Avoid getting any vinegar into your pet's eyes.

REMOVING TEAR DUCT STAIN FROM WHITE-HAIRED DOGS

I read with interest a report from the owner of a white bulldog with dark tear stains running from his tear duct area down. After various other suggested remedies which were not effective, the owner was told by a vet that the tear stains were caused by the acidity in the dog's system. His suggestion was to put vinegar in the dog's drinking water. He suggested putting just a few drops of vinegar in the drinking water for a few days and then increasing the amount of vinegar to about a teaspoon each day. Within a few weeks, the tear stains were gone for good!

SKIN AND COAT CONDITIONER

For skin infections, bath your dog and then rinse him with a solution of 1 part cider vinegar to 3 parts water.

125 ml (⅕ pint) of vinegar to a litre (2 pints) of water sprayed on to the coat of a horse or dog works like a vinegar hair rinse. Their coats gleam, providing an extremely economical alternative to expensive products.

PREVENTING DOGS FROM SCRATCHING

Keep dogs from scratching their ears by applying a few drops of vinegar to their drinking water.

ADDING CIDER VINEGAR AS A SUPPLEMENT
FOR YOUR DOG

Cider vinegar has the ability to prevent the growth of bacteria and mould. Therefore, adding it to your dog's fresh foods as a nutritional supplement has an additional purpose. The acid content of the vinegar will help reduce the chance of bacterial or fungal growth on fresh foods during the period of time they are in your dog's food bowl.

Apple cider vinegar has many outstanding qualities that are beneficial to pets in general, and dogs are no exception. Many vitamins, minerals and other nutrients and substances are available in cider vinegar to improve the health of your dog. Be sure to purchase organic unfiltered, unpasteurized cider vinegar. You'll know you've found the right stuff if you see sediment, referred to as the 'mother of vinegar', on the bottom of the bottle.

TRAINING YOUR DOG TO BEHAVE

Try solution of ½ vinegar and ½ water in a spray bottle. If your dog is disobedient, spray him, and he will soon do as he is told.

TREATING MINOR WOUNDS AND INFECTIONS
IN YOUR PET

Vinegar inhibits the growth of unfriendly bacteria in the digestive tract. It has detoxifying properties, strengthens the immune system and may relieve viral, bacterial and fungal infections. It is used as an antibacterial medicine and has a natural antibiotic effect. If applied topically to wounds and burns it will decrease the pain and promote healing.

CLEANING YOUR PET'S EARS
Mix ⅓ rubbing alcohol, ⅓ white vinegar and ⅓ water. Store in any old clean dropper bottle and use it to clean out your pet's ears. It works fine on dogs and cats. A vet's tip from years ago was to squirt 8–10 drops in the ear, holding the head to the side. Let it stand in the ear for a few seconds, then drain. Holding the animal's head tilted, massage the ear around in a circle, then tilt and wipe out with tissue. Apply once a month or if they are ear-scratching.

Warning: If applied daily for 3 days and the animal is still scratching or rubbing its ears, see a vet; they may have mites or a bacterial infection.

ELIMINATING CAT LITTER BOX ODOURS
When you clean the litter box, rinse it out and pour about 1 cm (½ in) of cheap white vinegar in the box. Let it stand for 20 minutes or so, then swish it around, rinse with cold water, and dry the box. The acid in the vinegar neutralizes the ammonia smell.

VINEGAR FOR RABBIT BREEDING
If your doe is unreceptive for breeding, add one tablespoon of white vinegar to her fresh water. After 24 hours the doe will be very receptive, and the buck will be happy too!

REDUCING SWELLINGS ON LEGS OF HORSES AND OTHER ANIMALS
For reducing the swelling on a horse (or any animal), wrap the leg in a rag soaked in cider vinegar. Wrap in plastic and then bandage to hold it in place. Leave on for 4 or more hours.

REDUCING BITES TO HORSES FROM FLIES
Add approximately five teaspoons of cider vinegar to your horse's oats, morning and evening, to dramatically reduce fly bites.

KEEPING FLIES AWAY FROM HORSES
Mix ⅓ vinegar (any type, but cider vinegar smells better), ⅓ water, and ⅓ bath oil in a spray bottle. This makes a good fly spray for horses and other animals — dogs, goats, etc — as well as barn spray to keep flies down.

VINEGAR FOR GOATS
Some goat owners add apple cider vinegar to their goats' water all year around. It seems to repel flies in the summer and prevents the water from freezing as fast in the winter. Add about two tablespoons to each 20 litre (5 gallon) bucket. Far from giving the milk an 'off' flavour, there seem to be no ill effects.

VINEGAR FOR CHICKENS
Add vinegar to chickens' water, especially in the winter, to keep them laying better and staying healthy. If your chickens don't have access to wild, natural food, give it to them all year round.

PREVENTING CHICKENS FROM PECKING
Stop chickens from pecking one another by adding a small dose of cider vinegar to their drinking water.

TENDERIZING POULTRY
Produce tender meat from your chickens by adding vinegar to poultry water.

INCREASING EGG PRODUCTION
Repeat method above.

CLEANING ANIMAL WATER CONTAINERS
Use white or cider vinegar to clean out the chickens' or pets' water containers which are left outside. Pour a small amount in the container, take a rag and wash the gunky parts and rinse. It keeps the water containers clean and fresh. Repeat once a month.

CLEANING RABBIT LITTER BOXES

White vinegar is the best cleaner for rabbit litter boxes. If it's used each time the litter box is cleaned, it keeps them like new. If there is already a build-up of dried urine in the box, scrubbing with vinegar will get rid of it.

CLEANING FISH TANKS

Use white vinegar to clean the mineral deposits that accumulate at the top of your fish aquarium. Soak a paper towel in the vinegar and simply wipe around the inside of the tank where the water has evaporated and left the white mineral deposits. You can also use it to clean aquarium ornaments. It is harmless to fish, so you don't need to worry if some of the vinegar happens to get into the water.

Home Decorating & Renovating

REMOVING GLUE FROM OLD FURNITURE
To loosen old glue around rungs and joints of tables and chairs under repair, apply distilled vinegar with a small oil can.

REMOVING GRIME FROM FURNITURE
Dirt and grime can be easily removed from woodwork with a solution of 275 ml (¼ pint) of ammonia, 150 ml (⅕ pint) of distilled vinegar, and 30 g (1 oz) of bicarbonate of soda dissolved in warm water. This solution will not dull the finish or leave streaks. Be careful of the smell when you mix these together.

FABRIC AND LEATHER GLUE
Vinegar makes excellent fabric/leather glue.

1 sachet clear gelatine
3 tbsp white vinegar
3–4 tbsp water
1 tsp glycerine

Melt the gelatine and water on a low heat, then add the other ingredients and mix well. Apply while warm. Store the remaining glue in a small plastic or glass jar. Warm it up next time before use.

SOFTENING PAINTBRUSHES
Soak a paint brush in hot vinegar, then wash out with warm, soapy water to soften it up.

CLEANING VARNISHED WOOD
If varnished wood has taken on a cloudy appearance but the cloudiness hasn't gone through to the wood, it can be removed by rubbing the wood with a soft cloth soaked in a solution of one tablespoon of distilled vinegar in a litre (2 pints) of luke-warm water. Wring out the cloth and rub into the wood. Complete the job by wiping the surface with a soft dry cloth.

REMOVING RING STAINS

Stubborn rings left where wet glasses have been placed on wood furniture can be removed by rubbing them with a mixture of equal parts of distilled vinegar and olive oil. Rub with the grain and polish for the best results.

CLEANING WOODEN PANELLING

Clean wood panelling with a mixture of one part olive oil to two parts of distilled vinegar in 1 litre (2 pints) of warm water. Moisten a soft cloth with the solution and wipe the panelling. The yellowing is then removed by wiping with a soft, dry cloth.

BASIC WOOD CLEANING SOLUTION

This is a good mix for well-used furniture. The vinegar works wonderfully to pull dirt out of wood.

3 tbsp white distilled vinegar
3 tbsp water
$\frac{1}{2}$ tsp liquid soap or detergent
A few drops of olive oil

Combine the ingredients in a bowl, saturate a sponge with the mixture, and squeeze out the excess to wash surfaces. The smell of vinegar will disappear in a few hours.

Always store carefully in a labelled jar or bottle.

CLEANING RAW WOOD

White vinegar can also be used to clean raw wood, such as a wooden cutting board. Pour straight vinegar on to the wood and then use a sponge to literally push the dirt away. Be sure to wipe in the direction of the wood grain, starting at one end and working to the other. This way the dirt you are trying to get rid of won't be pushed back into the wood grain.

PREVENTING PLASTER FROM DRYING OUT TOO QUICKLY

Prevent plaster from drying too quickly when patching or filling in by adding one tablespoon of vinegar to the water when mixing. This will slow the drying time.

HAND CARE AFTER PLASTER OR CLAY WORK

This tip came from a professional artist. You can rebalance the pH of the alkali in the material if you wash your hands with soap then rinse well with a one-to-one solution of white vinegar and water each time.

WALLPAPER PASTE SOLVENT

Vinegar makes a great solvent for wallpaper paste. Just dilute 275 ml (½ pint) of white vinegar with 2–3 litres (4 pints) of very warm water, and apply generously with a sponge. Once you get an edge or corner of the wallpaper to lift, then start working the vinegar solution behind the paper to break down the adhesive. This process is most effective when you keep your work area very damp — let the warmth of the water and the chemical properties of the vinegar do the work for you.

Rinse your sponge often and mix a new batch of vinegar and water solution when it becomes cool and/or murky. The bonus is that vinegar is inexpensive and it will not stain or discolour carpeting or other flooring.

REVIVING OLD LEATHERWORK

Mix 200 ml (⅓ pint) of vinegar with 400 ml (⅔ pint) of linseed oil. Shake this in a bottle until it reaches the consistency of cream. Rub into the leather and polish with a soft cloth.

REVIVING AN OLD STOVE OR FIREPLACE
All grease spots must be washed off and any rust removed, and the stove must be cold. Mix black-lead with vinegar to a creamy consistency and apply to the metal areas of the stove or fireplace. Polish with a stiff brush when nearly dry.

PREPARATION FOR PAINTING
Wiping down clean metal surfaces with a vinegar solution (1 part vinegar to 5 parts water) prepares the surface for painting, and reduces the incidence of peeling.

REMOVING TEMPERA PAINT
Vinegar works well to remove tempera paint, like you use when you decorate your windows for Christmas. It takes it off almost immediately. Sponge vinegar over the paint then wipe off, removing residual paint with paper towelling.

Miscellaneous Uses

CLEANING SPECTACLES

Eyeglasses will clean up and be free of streaks when wiped down with water to which a splash of vinegar has been added. (Note: Rum works well too!)

SMOOTHER NAIL VARNISH

Nail polish will go on smoother and stay on longer, if you clean your fingernails with white vinegar before applying the polish.

SHOE CLEANER

Remove winter salt stains from shoes by wiping with a cloth dampened in a vinegar solution. Use one tablespoon of vinegar to 275 ml (½ pint) of water.

GETTING RID OF FRUIT FLIES

Put a bowl of cider vinegar out to attract fruit flies. The same can be achieved by washing the windows with cider vinegar, but that's probably not the effect you want.

If this just attracts the flies but doesn't kill them, put one teaspoon of sugar, two teaspoons of cider vinegar and several drops of washing up liquid in a small shallow plastic container. Fill up with water. The flies are attracted to the vinegar, but the soap kills them.

Alternatively, take a small bowl and partially fill it with vinegar, then wrap it in cling film. Poke a few pinholes in the plastic wrap, and the fruit flies will fly in, but can't get out. Place the bowl wherever you see the fruit flies.

PERKING UP CUT FLOWERS

Keep cut flowers fresh longer by adding two tablespoons of vinegar and one tablespoon of sugar to each litre (2 pints) of water.

BIODEGRADEABLE BUG AND FLY SPRAY
Spraying bugs inside the home means that you get chemicals on carpets and furniture. Try filling an old water pistol with vinegar. You can then spray the offending insect without damaging the décor. This is alleged to work on cockroaches as well.

CLEANING DENTURES
To clean dentures leave them in vinegar for as long as you would leave them in a denture cleanser — about 15 minutes to half an hour. Then brush them thoroughly.

PREVENTING FADING OF EMBROIDERY THREAD
Dip the whole skein of thread in white vinegar and then air-dry. This sets the dye and when washing an embroidered item, there will be no running of colours.

CLEANING SILK FLOWER ARRANGEMENTS
Use a spray bottle filled with vinegar. When they get dusty, spray them lightly, and the dust is gone. They also look brand new!

REMOVING A PERFUME YOU DON'T LIKE
It is generally recommended in the trade that vinegar removes the smell of a perfume you don't like. Just apply it to the skin that has been sprayed with the undesired perfume.

NEW WICKS
Soak new propane lantern wicks in vinegar for several hours. Let them dry before using. The wicks will burn longer and brighter.

RUBBER CHICKEN
I can't think of a good reason for doing this, other than to demonstrate the scientific versatility of vinegar, or for a laugh, but apparently you can turn a chicken bone into rubber by soaking it in a glass of vinegar for three days. It will bend like rubber. Must try that sometime!

REMOVING STICKERS
Remove stickers by soaking a cloth in vinegar and covering for several minutes until the vinegar soaks in. The stickers should then peel off easily.

SHINY PATENT LEATHER
Patent leather will shine better if you wipe it with a soft cloth which has been moistened with distilled vinegar.

DOCTOR WHO
Vinegar is the only 'weapon' that can kill the mythical Slitheen!

Appendices

APPENDIX 1
HISTORICAL USES OF VINEGAR

Wound treatment (World WarI)
Treated rashes/bites/minor ailments
Preservative (Babylonians)
Beverage (Roman Legionnaires)
Cleopatra's bet (dissolved pearl)
Medicine (Hippocrates)
Natural by-product of alcoholic drinks:
   Beer/wine/other spirits
Condiment (Sumerians)
Preservative
Antibiotic
Detergent
Antiseptic
Haroseth
Medicinal benefits (Ancient Greece)
Aristotle documented it
Aided Hannibal's elephants
Turned stones soft and crumbly,
   a chemical bulldozer
Romans drank 'posca'
Brewed in Egyptian burial tombs
Leonardo Da Vinci (passed secret messages)
The Da Vinci Code: vinegar dissolved papyrus
Alchemists used it (accelerated its production)
Vine shoots, brambles and fish tongues added
   to vinegar wine
Chencu
Balsamic vinegar (Henry III)
Vinegar makers made a corporation
Plague potion
Killed germs on coins
Vinegar of four thieves (protection from plague
   when robbing bodies of plague victims):
   mixed with herbs/rosemary/sage to make
   this potion
Food preservation
Industrial revolution
Pasteurization
Commercial production

APPENDIX 2
SCIENTIFIC USES OF VINEGAR

Reacts with bacteria to become acetic acid
Refrigerated beer becomes vinegar
Can be made from beer or ale
Orleans method
Process of acetification
Sweet or sour uses:
   Malt vinegar
   Sugar vinegar
Commercially produced vinegars
Alernative vinegars, made from:
   Fruit juices
   Syrups
   Honey
   Molasses
   Cane sugar
Industrial vinegar (Ethyl alcohol)
By-product of paper industry (binder in papers)
Combining with wild yeast
Home brewing
Dressing salads
General-purpose usage
Pickling
Canning
No refrigeration needed
Makes cellulose
Acts on metals
Produces pigments useful for art
Used in 16th century alchemy
Vinegar paper
Oil spill clean-up sponge
Absorptive base for toxic material removal
Petroleum
Mining
Mineral and oil recovery
Clothing and shoes
Artificial leather products
One-piece textiles
Water purification
Audio products

APPENDIX 2
SCIENTIFIC USES OF VINEGAR (CONT.)

Audio speaker diaphragms
Forest products
Artificial wood strengthener
Filler for paper
High-strength containers
Speciality papers
Archival document repair
Paper base for long-lived currency
Aircrafts
Car bodies
Airplane structural elements
Rocket casings
Artificial arteries/vessels/skin

APPENDIX 3
PET AND ANIMAL USES OF VINEGAR

Removing fleas
Removing tear duct stain
Rearing goats
Rabbit breeding
Chicken breeding
Reducing swelling on legs of horses
Reducing bites to horses
Keeping flies away from horses
Cleaning fish tanks
Skin and coat conditioner
Clean animal water containers
Eliminating litter box odours
Cleaning rabbit litter boxes
Dog obedience training
Cleaning a pet's ears
Cider vinegar as a supplement
Treating minor wounds and infections
Preventing chickens from pecking
Preventing ear-scratching
Producing tender meat
Increasing egg production in poultry

APPENDIX 4
LAUNDRY USES OF VINEGAR

Label remover
Underarm mark removal
Underarm odour removal
Cleaning collars
Cleaning cuffs
Fabric softener
Stain remover
Terry nappies (diapers):
    Stain prevention
    Nappy rash prevention
    Lowering washing costs
Cutting down lint on clothing
Preventing colours from running
Removing tar from jeans
Removing stiffness from jeans
Removing hem marks
Preventing fading of laundry
Dyeing
Reducing ironing shine marks
Removing and setting creases
Cleaning/refreshing ironing board
Steam iron cleaner
Cleaning base of iron
Making blankets soft and fluffy
Removing smell of bleach
Removing cola stains
Removing grease from suede
Removing smoke smells
Deodorizing wool
Removing excess laundry suds

APPENDIX 5
OUTDOOR USES OF VINEGAR

Killing slugs
Removing brown patches from lawns
Antibacterial garden aid
Treating scratches
Removing stains from flowerpots
Discouraging ants
Weed suppressant
Controlling perennials
Killing weeds with boiling vinegar
Repelling mosquitoes
Ripening melons without mould
Keeping cats out of sandtrays
Increasing soil acidity
Neutralizing garden lime
Dissolving chewing gum
Cleansing septic tank
Keeping flies away from a pool
Cleaning windows
Removing spots from windows
Drain cleaner
Breaking down fatty acids
As a wood stain
Removing rust from bolts/screws/nails/hinges
Removing paint from glass
Removing calcium build-up from brickwork
Removing diesel smells
Cleaning windscreens
Removing lime deposits from windscreens
Preventing ice
Chrome polish
Grass killer
Removing stains on concrete
Keeping cats away
Helping growth of azaleas
Prolonging lives of flowers
Increasing soil acidity
Outdoor sports
Disposable tents and camping gear

APPENDIX 6
USING VINEGAR FOR HOME DECORATING AND RENOVATING

Removing glue from old furniture
Removing grime from furniture
Fabric and leather glue
Softening paintbrushes
Cleaning varnished wood
Removing ring stains
Cleaning wood panelling
Basic wood cleaning solution
Cleaning raw wood
Preventing plaster from drying out too quickly
Hand care after plastering
Wallpaper paste solvent
Reviving old leatherwork
Reviving old stoves
Reviving fireplaces
Preparation for painting
Removing tempera paint

APPENDIX 7
MISCELLANEOUS USES OF VINEGAR

Cleaning spectacles
Creating smoother nail varnish
Shoe cleaner
Getting rid of fruit flies
Perking up cut flowers
Biodegradable bug and fly spray
Cleaning dentures
Preventing thread from fading
Cleaning silk flowers
Removing perfume smells
New wicks
Rubberizing chicken bones
Removing stickers
Shiny patent leather
Drew out Beth's fever in *Little Women*
Used in *Doctor Who* to kill the 'Slitheen'

APPENDIX 8
USING VINEGAR FOR CLEANING
AND ODOUR CONTROL

General applications
    in cleaning
White vinegar contains
    specialized cleaners
Money-saving
Cleaning/sanitizing
    agent
Reduces:
    Bacteria
    Moulds
    Yeasts
Reduces E-coli on
    countertop surfaces:
    Laminate/wood/tile/
    concrete/stainless
    steel/granite
Reduces micro-organisms
Reduces mineral
    deposits
Prevents milk stone
    build-up
Used in construction
    industry
Rinsing walls and
    ceilings
Easy to dispense
    and control
Does not leave residues
Clean smell
Environmentally friendly
Removes coffee and
    tea stains
Loosens tough stains
Brightens stainless steel
Removes stains
    from pots
Removes fruit stains
Oven cleaner
Cleans kettles

Rinses dishes
Rinsing in the
    dishwasher
Microwave cleaner
Reviving kitchen cloths
Cleaning waste-disposal
    units
Cleaning chopping
    boards
Cleaning work surfaces
Cleaning out coffee
    maker
Grease cutter
Cleaning decanters/
    bottles/refrigerators
Refreshing ice trays
Sweet-smelling
    bread box
Cleaning solutions
Floor cleaner
Window wash
Cleaning copper
    and brass
Cleaning metal screens
Cleaning aluminium
    furniture
Cleaning drains
Cleaning tarnished
    copper
Floor cleaner
Vinyl floor cleaner
Carpet spot/stain
    remover
Waxing a floor
Removing water stains
    from leather
Reviving leather
    upholstery
Cleaning whirlpool tub

Cleaning fireplace doors
Toilet cleaner
Cleaning shower head
Cleaning lime deposits
Cleaning porcelain
  enamel
Cleaning baths
Cleaning sinks
Cleaning fittings
Removing hard water
  deposits
Furniture polish
Brassware
Removing rust from
  cast iron
Removing rust from
  antiques
Aromatic air freshener
Removing paint fumes
Removing cooking odours
Removing the smell
  of onions
Sponge restorer
Hand cleaner
Removing vomit smells
Removing sour milk
  smells
Removing stale smoke
  smells
Removing perfume
  smells
Removing animal urine
  smells
Cleaning humidifiers
Cleaning photocopier
  glass
Cleaning plastic shower
  curtains
Cleaning plastics
Removing oil stains
Carpet cleaners
Cleaning lunchboxes/
  bread boxes

Cleaning dishwasher
  glasses
Removing refrigerator
  smells
Rubbish disposal
Deodorizing jars
Cleaning bottles
Cleaning hot plates
Cleaning fine china
Cleaning oven vents
Cleaning barbecue grills
Rust dissolver
Sticker removal
Fabric glue
Removing dust on fans
Removing coke stains
Removing soap residue
Restoring hairbrushes
De-staticing plastics
Wallpaper remover
Remedying sagging
  cane bamboo
Prolonging lifespan
  of tights
Cleaning unsightly film
  in bottles
Killing germs in
  bathroom
Increasing paint's
  adherence to
  galvanized metals
Reducing mineral
  deposits in pipes,
  kettles and tanks
Making soap, when
  combined with
  bicarbonate of soda
  (baking soda)
Anti-fogging glass
  cleaner

APPENDIX 9
USING VINEGAR FOR HEALTH AND PERSONAL CARE

Cider vinegar has nutritious qualities, increasing:
Phosphorus
Potassium
Sodium
Magnesium
Calcium
Sulphur
Iron
Fluorine
Silicon
Contributes to healthy veins/blood vessels/ arteries
Aids cleansing
Re-introduction of minerals
Clotting of the blood
Oxidation of the blood
Purifier
Breaks down fatty mucous
Promotes health of vital organs of the body
Prevents alkaline urine
Prevents high blood pressure
Neutralizes toxic substances
Apple cider vinegar:
Helps watery eyes
Sinus problems
Catarrhal problems
Bones and teeth
Abrasions
Reduces itch from poisons
Aftershave
After-sun treatment

Relieving swelling and fluid
Relieving age spots
Relieving allergy to dust mites
Assisting arthritis
Relieving asthma
Relieving athlete's foot
Removing boils
Alleviating sore bones/ bruises/stiffness/ swelling
Calcium supplement with egg shells
Cleansing lotion
Removes corns/calluses
Helps colds/cold sores
Alleviates constipation
Alleviates cramps
Removes colitis
Alleviates coughs/ tickly coughs
Diabetes
Diarrhoea
Natural deodorant
Alleviates depression
Alleviates dizziness
Removes ear discharge
Removes eczema
Soothes tired and sore eyes
Eases fatigue
Fights free radicals
Eases food poisoning
Helps gallstones/ kidney stones
Eases haemorrhoids
Hair care
Hair rinse
Hay fever

Headaches
Headlice
Heart
Heartburn
Healing wounds
Stopping hiccoughs
Lowering high blood
  pressure
Stopping hot flushes
Easing indigestion
Easing bloating
Aiding infected
  ear piercings
Repelling insects
Curing insomnia
Easing irritable bowels
Flushing kidneys and
  bladder
Helping menopause
  symptoms
Metabolism
Killing off unwanted
  bacteria
Treating minor burns
Sore muscles
Nasal congestion
Nausea
Nose bleeds
Pedicure pampering
Reducing cholesterol
Skin rashes
Sore throat
Sprains
Stiff joints
Stings
Tanning aid
Tendonitis
Removing toenail fungus
Easing toothaches
Treating ulcers
Treating varicose veins
Removing warts
Weight loss

Whitening teeth
Yeast infections
Anti-dandruff
Treating acne
Brittle/soft nails
Swollen/chapped skin
Foot odour
Serum cholesterol
  reduction
Removing fruit stains
  from hands
Detecting cervical
  cancer
Baby care products
Disposable recyclable
  nappies (diapers)
Wound care dressings
Drug delivery agents
Artificial skin substrates
Cosmetics and beauty
Skin creams
Astringents
Base for artificial nails
Thickener and
  strengthener for
  fingernail polish
Relieves mosquito itch

USES OF SPECIFIC TYPES OF VINEGAR

MALT VINEGAR

Flavours beer
Enhances taste with:
Peppercorns
Allspice
Cloves
Chillies
Pickling onions
Pickling walnuts
Making piccalilli
Flavours watery
vegetables/cabbage
Fish and chips
(French fries)
Absorbs excess fat
Used for mundane jobs:
Cleaning glass
Coffee pots
Detergent
Disinfectant

SPIRIT/RED WINE VINEGAR

Used as distilled vinegar
Flavoured with:
Honey
Spices
Flower petals
Seaweed
Cabernet Sauvignon
Merlot
Pinot Noir
Raspberry
Used in:
Fruit salads
Marinades
Basting
Salad Dressings

WHITE WINE/CHAMPAGNE VINEGAR

Hollandaise sauce
Béarnaise sauce
Vinaigrettes
Soups
Stews
Sweetness in melons
Spicy salsas
Replaces cream/butter
Dresses delicate salads
Sublime vinaigrette

CIDER VINEGAR

Medicinal uses
Fruit salads
Base for herb vinegars

WHITE VINEGAR

Various household uses
Can be combined with:
Thyme
Rosemary
Basil
Garlic
Peppercorns
Balances flavours
without adding fat
Reduces need for salt
Deepens taste of
the dish

RICE/CHENCU VINEGAR

Used in Asian dishes
Makes aromatic oriental
dishes
Used for flavouring
Contains amino acids
Used for:
Calcium
Iron
Zinc
Manganese
Flavours fruit, stir-fries,
herbs and spices
Soups
Pickling
Chicken dishes
Fish dishes
Coconut vinegars in
Thai dishes.

BLACK RICE VINEGAR
Substitute for black
   vinegar
Dipping sauce
Noodles
Soup
Seafood dishes
Shark's fin soup
Sushi
Salad dressings
Vegetable dressings
Hot and sour sauce

SHERRY VINEGAR
Sprinkle over:
   Salads
   Cooked vegetables
Accompanies:
   Duck
   Beef
   Game

BALSAMIC VINEGAR
Desserts
Digestifs
Added to gravies
Acquired as gifts
Cooked meats
Season green salads
Strawberries
Peaches
Melons
Shavings of parmesan
Dressings for gravadlax
Tuna carpaccio

FRUIT VINEGARS
Cooking duck
Cooking ham
Complementing fruits
   and salads
Pineapple vinegar as a
   substitute to cider
   vinegar
Tokyo Fruit vinegars:
   Lychee
   Raspberry
   Cranberry
   Mango
   Apple
   Rosehip

CANE VINEGAR
Pickling
Mustards
Vinaigrettes
Adds flavour to:
   Herring
   Sauces
   Sweet-and-sour dishes
   Sauerbraten

UMEBOSHI VINEGAR
Dips
Salad dressings
Flavouring steamed
   vegetables

APPENDIX 11 - CULINARY USES OF VINEGAR

VEGETARIAN/HERB DISHES
Vinegar, bread and herbs
An addition to marinades
Diet vinaigrettes
De-gassing beans
Rinsing fruit and vegetables
Avocado and tomato salad
Avocado and mozarella salad
French bread canapés
Goat cheese
Asparagus appetizer
French dressing
Sweet-and-sour salad dressing
Sherry vinegar and mustard
    dressing
Mint and honey salad dressing
Mayonnaise
Sesame seed and raspberry
    dressing
Italian dressing with sour cream
Potato salad
Parsley, sage, rosemary and
    thyme vinegar
Tarragon vinegar
Camp vinegar
Basil and cinammon vinegar
Sage and caraway vinegar
Jalapeño garlic vinegar

Celery vinegar
Cress vinegar
Cherokee vinegar
Chilli vinegar
Cucumber vinegar
Escaveeke sauce
Spiced vinegar
Shallot vinegar
Garlic/shallot pickle
Pickled onions
Piccalilli
Raspberry vinegar
Asian black bean and
    asparagus salad
Autumn broccoli salad
Texas blue cheese slaw
Hummus in pitta pockets
Pickled relish platter
Herbed olives and onion
    marinade
Vinegar cheese

MEAT/FISH DISHES
Fish and chips (French fries)
Tasty boiled ham
Tender boiled beef
Meat soup stock
Marinade for kebabs

Apricot barbecue sauce
Oriental marinade and
    baste for beef
Marinade for chicken
Marinade for slowly cooking
    brisket
Roast salmon with balsamic
    glaze
Chicken with malt vinegar
Chicken salad with raspberry
    vinegar
Strawberry vinegars:
Basting sauce for chicken/
    duck/pork
Bon bon chicken salad
Skewered chicken breast with
    Italian salsa verde
Vinegar pies
Chicken adobo
Salmon with onion marmalade
Country French caviar

DESSERTS
Strawberries balsamico
Melon sorbet
Vinegar cookies
Tangy lemon custard tart
Thicker ice cream

DIETING/JUICES
Kombucha elixir
Manchurian tea
Salad dressing for dieters
Go-go juice
Alternative to lemon juice
Health drinks
Low-calorie crisps (potato
    chips), dips and sweets

GENERAL COOKING TRICKS
Tenderizing meat
Peeling hard-boiled eggs
Boiled eggs with no cracks
Colour enhancer
Fluffier meringue
Poaching eggs
Keeping cheese fresh
Whiter fish
Buttermilk
Removing fish scales
Firmer gelatine and jelly
Using up the ketchup
Removing bugs from lettuce
Reducing starch in pasta/rice
Substitute for sour milk
Substitute for eggs

Preserving sour cream
Boil vinegar to preserve:
    Eggs
    Oysters
    Onions
    Tomatoes
    Mushrooms
    Lemons
    Limes
    Melons
Boost taste of scrambled eggs
Fluffier rice
Shiny crust on home-made
    bread
Ham cooking and preservation
Preventing discoloration of
    peeled potatoes
Pepper preservation
Stopping lumpy icing
Taking the edge off your
    appetite
Tender fish
Shiny crust on pies
Making cauliflower white
    and clean
Base for artificial meat
Sausage and meat casing
Thickening salad dressing